LETS
GO
PUBLISH

Dedication

I dedicate this book

To my wonderful brothers and sisters:

Angel Edward J. Kelly, Jr.

Nancy "Ann" Flannery

Mary A. Daniels

Joseph A. Kelly

I surely am a lucky person to have

Such wonderfulness in the family of

Edward J Kelly and Irene McKeown Kelly

.

Acknowledgments:

I appreciate all the help that I have received in putting this book together as well as all of the other 147 books from the past.

My acknowledgments were so large at one time that readers complained that they had to go through too many pages to get to page one.

And, so I put my acknowledgment list online, and it continues to grow. Believe it or not, it now costs about a dollar less to print my books. No kidding!

Thank you and God bless you all for your help. Please check out www.letsgopublish.com to read the latest version of my heartfelt acknowledgments updated for this book.

In this book, I received some extra special help from many fine American patriots including Dennis Grimes, Gerry Rodski, Wily Ky Eyely, Angel Irene McKeown Kelly, Angel Edward Joseph Kelly Sr., Angel Edward Joseph Kelly Jr., Ann Flannery, Angel James Flannery Sr., Mary Daniels, Bill Daniels, Robert Gary Daniels, Angel Sarah Janice Daniels, Angel Punkie Daniels, Joe Kelly, Diane Kelly, Brian P. Kelly, Mike P. Kelly, Katie P. Kelly, Angel Ben Kelly, and Budmund (Buddy) Arthur Kelly.

Thank you all!

Table of Contents

Preface:

Well, I knew that I was voting for Donald Trump as soon as he broke through the pack of Republicans and began his showdowns with his real opponent, Hillary Clinton. Like many Democrats, I had had enough of the Clintons, but my predilection to Trump was more because of him and not because of Clinton. It had more to do with the fact that he reminded me of a last man standing in the way of a country ready to go off a big cliff.

At the end of the day, when the dust had settled, and the battle was over, the last man standing won. Donald Trump won the election despite all odds. In many ways he got elected because he was the last man standing between an Obama-American hell-hole and a return to the Promised Land of our founders.

He represents a welcome change from establishment elitist politics. His great ideas for solving the issues facing America today lined up with the thinking of most Americans who were paying attention and who were annoyed at the prior administration.

I am glad that you are reading this book, so you too can understand why Donald Trump was not just a default choice for President. I wrote an essay early in the campaign titled, God gave us Donald Trump. I stand by that thought even after the Democrats continue to add Russian characters into their daily soap opera trying to replay and undo the 2016 election. Democrat shenanigans are getting old. I have never been more pleased with a vote than my vote for Donald J. Trump.

He is a great man and he is already becoming a great president for you, me, and all those who love America. He knows business and we are already experiencing an enlivened economy. With substantial foreign business experience, he is setting America up as the top dog in the world, and as expected, he is making no apologies.

Trump is a tough American, so we can count on not being pushed around in foreign affairs or delicate negotiations. Our new president as expected, is a winner all the way around. He hates to lose and seldom does. America is very happy that we now have someone in charge who believes we can win.

The weaknesses of the Republican Party came out in spades in the primary season and continued as weak-kneed RINO such as Jeb Bush, John Kasich, Lindsey Graham, John McCain decided to become tools for the Democrats. During the campaign Donald Trump did not even give them lip service.

In his own way, Mr. Trump told them and all the establishment elites where to go. I like that. These RINOs and their Marxist friends across the aisle had been destroying America for their own benefit. It took a guy with guts and stamina to beat them. The last man standing stood against them and won a great victory for the people.

Donald Trump first whooped everybody who was anybody in the GOP. He then ran against a person that some call a withered fascist-- Hillary Clinton. There were many Democrats like me who felt that we could not afford a liar in the White House. We were all in for Donald J. Trump.

For those who can ignore the media fake news and outright lies, there is plenty to admire about President Trump. Watching his children in action at the GOP convention and the chemistry within the family, Americans got the full sense of what a fine man and a fine dad he is.

America needs Donald Trump—a businessman and a great negotiator to compete in the world, not somebody like the former president who unfortunately for the country found business as a necessary evil. Barack Obama chose to have nothing to do with sound business principles while being in charge of the US economy. Hillary Clinton was ready to be more of the same—a third Termo of Obama.

The former president gave the impression for years that he had true disdain for America and Americans. It was like he would have loved all Americans to give up their freedoms and become government dependents. I am convinced he would have liked America to give up its position as #1 in the world. Trump is clearly for America and Americans-First and he demonstrated that in his nearly 400 huge campaign rallies. Trump was a Nationalist running as a Republican because it made business sense to not go third party.

Hillary was more like Obama -- socialistic and Marxist and she came off even more radical than Obama. For example, Hillary never seemed to be too keen on freedom. She likes her freedom for sure but not yours. She was working on eliminating the Bill of Rights and had already earmarked the # 1 and #2 Amendments of the Constitution for removal.

Yes, we were at the point in which a presidential candidate's position of not being actively opposed to the Bill of Rights was a key selling point for their candidacy.

The GOP today is still full of losers and babies who won't even keep their vows made in the pledge to support the Party's own nominee. No wonder the prior president was treated as an emperor. His sad agenda received no interference from the wimpy GOP. They quaked at the sight of Obama. Trump doesn't quake at anything.

For years, I have hoped that somebody such as Rush Limbaugh or Donald Trump or somebody with influence and power and money would come along to change our two-party system. I put my vision to words in two books, the first, written five years ago titled, Kill the Republican Party, and the second written this past summer titled It's Time for the John Doe Party.

The idea is to rid the party of the swamp and start over again with a new name such as The American Party or the John Doe Party, hoping to attract all current Republicans other than the swamp, and all Democrats who are like me, pro-American to a fault. It is still a dream yet for many like me we are watching the Republican Congress very closely.

For this ole conservative Democrat, the Republicans for years—even when my dad and I voted together before he died, always seemed to be the better choice than the far-left whacko Democrats. Yet, after Reagan, there were still bad choices and weak men.

Donald Trump has a lot of Reagan toughness and goodness in him. He has a great plan for America and in this book, we answer definitively the question of "Why Trump Got Elected!" First of all, he is the best choice. Second, he is honest. Third, he will keep his word and make America great again in ways in which Americans will all be so pleased. Trump is destined to be a great President.

America has more than one economic issue for sure, but it still is the best place to live on earth. Our nation is full to the brim with economic issues. When tackled one by one, they all can be solved and right now, they are works in process—being solved thanks to the new President. This book shows discusses the problems that during the Obama years prevented many people in American from having a good life. Donald Trump and Mike Pence have taken on the mission to make life better for all Americans

I sure hope you enjoy this book and I hope that it inspires you to continue to take action. Our Congress can certainly be more pro-American and more responsive to the people's needs and not their own. I hope the book in some ways helps you look at things differently. Our new president has settled in and he is already implementing a host of innovative items on his agenda. I hope you digest Trump's entire plan, be willing to adopt it, and add to it your own positive notions for building a better America. And, please do not trust the press to do your thinking for you.

Together, we can help make the US a far better country. We should smile as we accomplished our first and best objective. We electd Donald Trump as our president. Now, we must support his hard work and speak up to the Congress when they get in his way.

Brian W. Kelly, Author

About the Author

Brian W. Kelly is a retired Assistant Professor in the Business Information Technology (BIT) program at Marywood University, where he also served as the IBM i and midrange systems technical advisor to the IT faculty. Kelly developed and taught many college and professional courses in the IT and business areas. He is also a contributing technical editor to IT Jungle's "The Four Hundred" and "Four Hundred Guru" Newsletters.

A former IBM Senior Systems Engineer, he has an active consultancy in the information technology field, (www.kellyconsulting.com). He is the author of 147 other books and hundreds of articles about IT and topics about America.

Book #72 is called *Saving America The Trump Way* and has a number of suggestions that when added to Trump's own, can Make America Great Again.

Kelly is a frequent speaker at US events such as COMMON, IBM conferences, and other technical conferences and computer user group meetings across the United States. Brian is always ready to accept invitations to speak at political rallies on behalf of conservative and nationalist candidates.

Brian ran for Congress as a conservative Democrat in 2010, took no donations, and shook up the political world in Northeastern PA when he scored 17% of the vote in a three man-race.

Chapter 1 Michael Moore & Candidate Donald Trump

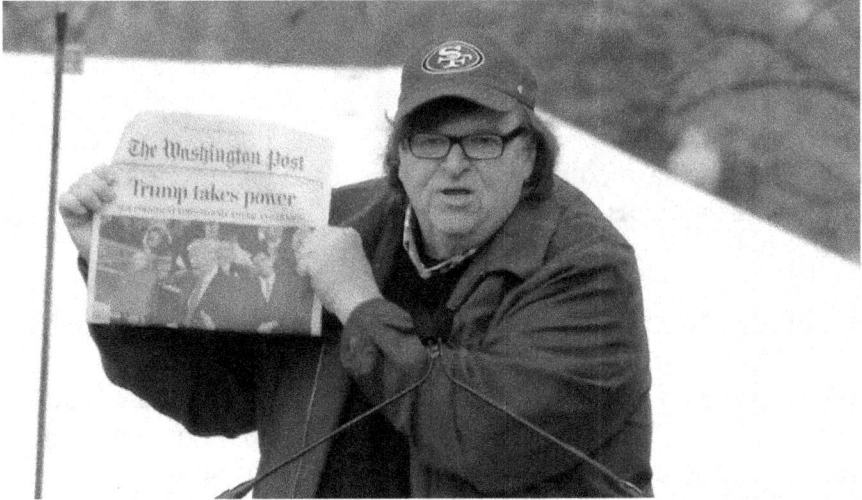

Was Candidate Trump destined to win?

As a Democrat, when Barack Obama beat Milk Toast Mitt Romney in 2008's presidential election, though I voted for Romney, I was not too terribly upset that Obama had won. Like everybody else I knew little about him, but he seemed to be quite eloquent in his speech and did not appear to have a race axe to grind.

The two-year Senator from Illinois had not distinguished himself in his political career and at that time, he had not extinguished himself, either. He could talk up a storm and he seemed like he would be a man in office who would preside fairly over America. I was not concerned initially.

Though from my eyes there was no blatant racism problem in the country for Obama to solve, I felt that the Obama presidency would really be post-racial. I was happy that our times were not like when we had race riots in the 1960's. Things had gotten lots better in America. I was pleased that with a man, who identified as a "black" president, who also understood the white world from his mother's side, we could finally put all of the ill-will about race from the past behind us.

My biggest surprise was that a "black man" would be so obviously biased on behalf of the black population. I was shocked to find President Obama to be one-sided towards blacks. I soon learned that whites had little chance in the new post-racial Obama presidency. From my eyes, race relations were Obama's first failure as president. I quickly learned that I could not trust him to do the right thing for America. I was very disappointed for eight years as from my eyes things in general, not just race, got worse, not better.

When Hillary Clinton promised four more years of Obama, I knew that I would do whatever I could to help somebody else become president. Donald Trump was not my favorite in the beginning, but he soon became my favorite as I learned that he would not be pushed around by anybody. I like to call my reaction to Trump when I finally understood him as a breath of fresh air.

To support him in his candidacy, in addition to sending in some checks and attending rallies, I wrote at least ten books and a number of letters to the editor in support of the Trump presidency. I gave my books away to anybody who wanted one and brought them to biker rallies such as one up above Scranton, PA in Dalton. At this rally sponsored by Chris Cox and the Bikers for Trump, I put a bunch of books out to help the cause. My most popular Trump for president book was about 240 pages and it was titled *Why Trump?* This book, "Why Trump Got Elected!" book in many ways is a follow-up to that popular book.

To show how I really felt about the Trump candidacy and to help others see things differently than what appeared to be the mainstream thought. I sent the following letter to the local paper, The Citizens' Voice. I titled it *God gave us Donald Trump.* I did not treat that notion lightly. The piece is short, so I have included it below:

> There are many billionaires who want things their way on taxes and they figure they will benefit if their lobbyists get to the right politician. Donald Trump is actually running for office as a

billionaire. He docs not need a job. Yet, he is investing a lot of time in America. He does not need it. But, if he is successful, his kids will grow up in America and he wants it to be the finest country of any possible country ever. Bravo, Donald Trump.

Mr. Trump wants it to be like the America as founded by honest founders. Donald Trump is intrinsically honest. He may round up on some issues in his favor, but he is not corrupt. He wants his kids to love him and respect him just like you want your kids to think of you.

We are only on Earth for a short time. Why should we not do our best? I love that Donald Trump, a billionaire who needs me like a hole in the head, thinks I matter. He thinks you matter. He thinks America matters. He thinks God matters. He is right on all points. Unlike you and me, he has the means and the opportunity to really show God and his family what a good man he really is.

We have been waiting for you, Mr. Trump, since Ronald Reagan left us. God gave us Donald Trump.

I am convinced that it is up to us to make him our president. We did not know how bad the Bushes were until they went into their recent crying tantrum because they lost. We just know that they were not too good when they had the power.

Donald Trump is bombastic, arrogant when he knows he is right, and he is often inartful in his speech when he is upset. However, he, like my father, is a very good man. I welcome the opportunity to cast my vote for him. I thank God for the opportunity.

Brian W. Kelly

After that little piece ran in the Citizens' Voice, nobody had to guess which candidate I was endorsing.

Like many others, I welcomed a change to times in which America was heralded and not put down. I longed for a period in which the Democratic Party and its minions would not parade around the world apologizing for America and Americans. As I saw Donald Trump, mostly on the US stage, giving his speeches and talking about making America great again, I was very encouraged.

Yet, I was ever fearful that the corrupt press would try to slant the opinion of many Americans to favor Mrs. Clinton over the bombastic Trump. That is exactly what they did—as if they were a branch of the Democratic Party instead of the Fourth Estate. h

At the time, I was unaware that Michael Moore, about whom I have little regard, had concerns just the opposite of mine. His biggest fear was that Donald Trump would become president of the United States.

Michael Moore predicted Trump's big win

Who is Michael Moore? Adrian Wooldridge of the Weekly Standard does an accurate job of describing Moore:

> THERE ARE MANY THINGS that can be said against Michael Moore. An odd combination of Howard Stern and Paul Krugman, Moore is the king of all left-wing media, from films to books, who specializes in trashing everything that conservative America holds dear. For Moore, businessmen are always trampling on the faces of the poor, Republicans are always the tools of sinister vested interests, and America is always up to no good in the world. But say this for the pudgy auteur, he has his uses as a timesaver at dinner parties in hyper-partisan America. If the woman next to you admires Moore, she probably dated Dean and is now firmly married to Kerry; if she regards Moore as a bilious blowhard, then she is probably going to vote for George W. Bush.

Michael Moore wrote this little piece on his web site offering five major reasons for his deep concern about Hillary's probable loss. To help liberal progressives, who are reading this book, know that I did my research, I present one of their own, Mike Moore, whose reasons why Trump would win were not at all off the mark. In many ways Michael Moore described in no uncertain terms "Why Trump Got Elected!"

I have reproduced it almost exactly as it was written on his site. Moore talked about five reasons why he thought Trump would win the election. Yet, in his stream of conscious style of writing he forgot to identify a few of his points. I found another article where he made the same points and I inserted them in his Web opening where they would have been if he was awake while he was writing. That is the only change I made so this is Michael Moore at his best / worst depending on your perspective.

You will see that Moore wrote this Web article in a caustic, sarcastic, nasty tone and he put down all Americans as losers and dummies if they favored Trump over Hillary. Nonetheless, he got it right—Trump was going to win—and there was nothing he could do about it.

Please try not to be offended if you are a pro-Trump guy like myself. He is hard on us for sure. We can take some solace as Moore was pre-feeling his pain as Trump had yet to win.. but Trump did win and that can make us all feel better about the future. Sorry MM. Here is Michael Moore in all his glory:

Friends:

I am sorry to be the bearer of bad news, but I gave it to you straight last summer when I told you that Donald Trump would be the Republican nominee for president. And now I have even more awful, depressing news for you: Donald J. Trump is going to win in November. This wretched, ignorant, dangerous part-time clown and full- time sociopath is going to be our next president. President Trump. Go ahead and say the words, 'cause you'll be saying them for the next four years: "PRESIDENT TRUMP."

Never in my life have I wanted to be proven wrong more than I do right now.

[Michael Moore is a nasty guy. Don't you think? What if it were Trump talking about Hillary or Obama or even Michael Moore? – A wretched, ignorant, dangerous part-time clown and full-time sociopath—can you imagine anybody calling Obama that?]

I can see what you're doing right now. You're shaking your head wildly – "No, Mike, this won't happen!" Unfortunately, you are living in a bubble that comes with an adjoining echo chamber where you and your friends are convinced the American people are not going to elect an idiot for president. You alternate between being appalled at him and laughing at him because of his latest crazy comment or his embarrassingly narcissistic stance on everything because everything is about him. And then you listen to Hillary and you behold our very first female president, someone the world respects, someone who is whip-smart and cares about kids, who will continue the Obama legacy because that is what the American people clearly want! Yes! Four more years of this!

[The mere thought of that last part would turn the stomachs of a lot of good Americans who had enough.]

You need to exit that bubble right now. You need to stop living in denial and face the truth which you know deep down is very, very real. Trying to soothe yourself with the facts – "77% of the electorate are women, people of color, young adults under 35 and Trump can't win a majority of any of them!" – or logic – "people aren't going to vote for a buffoon or against their own best interests!" – is your brain's way of trying to protect you from trauma. Like when you hear a loud noise on the street and you think, "oh, a tire just blew out," or, "wow, who's playing with firecrackers?" because you don't want to think you just heard someone being shot with a gun. It's the same reason why all the initial news and eyewitness reports on 9/11 said "a small plane accidentally flew into the World Trade Center." We want to – we need to – hope for the best because, frankly, life is already a shit show and it's hard enough struggling to get by from paycheck to paycheck. We can't handle much more bad news. So, our mental state goes to default when something scary is actually, truly happening. The first people plowed down by the truck in Nice spent their final moments on earth waving at the driver whom they thought had simply lost control of his truck, trying to tell him that he jumped the curb: "Watch out!," they shouted. "There are people on the sidewalk!"

Well, folks, this isn't an accident. It is happening. And if you believe Hillary Clinton is going to beat Trump with facts and smarts and logic, then you obviously missed the past year of 56 primaries and caucuses where 16 Republican candidates tried that, and every kitchen sink they could throw at Trump and nothing could stop his juggernaut. As of today, as things stand now, I believe this is going to happen – and in order to deal with it, I need you first to acknowledge it, and then maybe, just maybe, we can find a way out of the mess we're in.

[Yes, Mr. Moore. You were right. Donald Trump is now our President and it is because of nasty people like you not in spite of you.]

Don't get me wrong. I have great hope for the country I live in. Things are better. The left has won the cultural wars. Gays and lesbians can get married. A majority of Americans now take the liberal position on just about every polling question posed to them: Equal pay for women – check. Abortion should be legal – check. Stronger environmental laws – check. More gun control – check. Legalize marijuana – check. A huge shift has taken place – just ask the socialist who won 22 states this year. And there is no doubt in my mind that if people could vote from their couch at home on their X-box or PlayStation, Hillary would win in a landslide.

But that is not how it works in America. People have to leave the house and get in line to vote. And if they live in poor, Black or Hispanic neighborhoods, they not only have a longer line to wait in, everything is being done to literally stop them from casting a ballot. So, in most elections it's hard to get even 50% to turn out to vote. And therein lies the problem for November – who is going to have the most motivated, most inspired voters show up to vote? You know the answer to this question. Who's the candidate with the most rabid supporters? Whose crazed fans are going to be up at 5 AM on Election Day, kicking ass all day long, all the way until the last polling place has closed, making sure every Tom, Dick and Harry (and Bob and Joe and Billy Bob and Billy Joe and Billy Bob Joe) has cast his ballot? That's right. That's the high level of danger we're in. And don't fool yourself — no amount of compelling Hillary TV ads, or outfacting him in the debates or Libertarians siphoning votes away from Trump is going to stop his mojo.

Here are the 5 reasons Trump is going to win:

1. Midwest Math, or Welcome to Our Rust Belt Brexit. I believe Trump is going to focus much of his attention on the four blue states in the rustbelt of the upper Great Lakes – Michigan, Ohio, Pennsylvania and Wisconsin. Four traditionally Democratic states – but each of them have elected a Republican governor since 2010 (only Pennsylvania has now finally elected a Democrat). In the Michigan primary in March, more Michiganders came out to vote for the Republicans (1.32 million) that the Democrats (1.19 million). Trump is ahead of Hillary in the latest polls in Pennsylvania and tied with her in Ohio. Tied? How can the race be this close after everything Trump has said and done? Well maybe it's because he's said (correctly) that the Clintons' support of NAFTA helped to destroy the industrial states of the Upper Midwest. Trump is going to hammer Clinton on this and her support of TPP and other trade policies that have royally screwed the people of these four states. When Trump stood in the shadow of a Ford Motor factory during the Michigan primary, he threatened the corporation that if they did indeed go ahead with their planned closure of that factory and move it to Mexico, he would slap a 35% tariff on any Mexican-built cars shipped back to the United States. It was sweet, sweet music to the ears of the working class of Michigan, and when he tossed in his threat to Apple that he would force them to stop making their iPhones in China and build them here in America, well, hearts swooned, and Trump walked away with a big victory that should have gone to the governor next-door, John Kasich.

From Green Bay to Pittsburgh, this, my friends, is the middle of England – broken, depressed, struggling, the smokestacks strewn across the countryside with the carcass of what we use to call the Middle Class. Angry, embittered working (and nonworking) people who were lied to by the trickle-down of Reagan and abandoned by Democrats who still try to talk a good line but are really just looking forward to rub one out with a lobbyist from Goldman Sachs who'll write them nice big check before leaving the room. What happened in the UK with Brexit is going to happen here. Elmer Gantry shows up looking like Boris Johnson and just says whatever shit he can make up to convince the masses that this is their chance! To stick it to ALL of them, all who wrecked their American Dream! And now The Outsider, Donald Trump, has arrived to clean house! You don't have to agree with him! You don't even have to like him! He is your personal Molotov cocktail to throw right into the center of the bastards who did this to you! SEND A MESSAGE! TRUMP IS YOUR MESSENGER!

And this is where the math comes in. In 2012, Mitt Romney lost by 64 electoral votes. Add up the electoral votes cast by Michigan, Ohio, Pennsylvania and Wisconsin. It's 64. All Trump needs to do to win is to carry, as he's expected to do, the swath of traditional red states from Idaho to Georgia (states that'll never vote for Hillary Clinton), and then he just needs these four rust belt states. He doesn't need Florida. He doesn't need Colorado or Virginia. Just Michigan, Ohio, Pennsylvania and Wisconsin. And that will put him over the top. This is how it will happen in November.

[The following #s, 2, 3, & 4, were inserted here because Moore's stream of consciousness writing made him lose count of his five reasons.]

2. The Trump Family
Trump's main surrogates—his own family—have become Republican National Convention stars, and their testimonials

may cause voters to consider, "Well, if he raised them, he can't be so bad, right?" Moore points out that the family members are not really looking like the "hostages" liberal voters might have thought they would. In fact, "between [Melania] and the children, none of them have offered any of the sort of anecdotes that you would expect," Moore pointed out.

3. Make America Great Again? How About Just Reality Television

Moore believes Trump doesn't even want to be in the White House; that he'll give it to Mike Pence and his children after buying an estate in Fairfax. "The thing that we're describing... 'Make America Great Again'... He's gonna turn his presidency into a reality show; a literal reality show. But if I say that, millions are gonna go, f**k yeah," Moore said.

4. The Last Stand of the Angry White Man. Our male-

dominated, 240-year run of the USA is coming to an end. A woman is about to take over! How did this happen?! On our watch! There were warning signs, but we ignored them. Nixon, the gender traitor, imposing Title IX on us, the rule that said girls in school should get an equal chance at playing sports. Then they let them fly commercial jets. Before we knew it, Beyoncé stormed on the field at this year's Super Bowl (our game!) with an army of Black Women, fists raised, declaring that our domination was hereby terminated! Oh, the humanity!

That's a small peek into the mind of the Endangered White Male. There is a sense that the power has slipped out of their hands, that their way of doing things is no longer how things are done. This monster, the "Feminazi," the thing that as Trump says, "bleeds through her eyes or wherever she bleeds," has conquered us — and now, after having had to endure eight years of a black man telling us what to do, we're supposed to just sit back and take eight years of a woman bossing us around? After that it'll be eight years of the gays in the White House! Then the transgenders! You can see where this is going. By then animals will have been granted human rights and a f---in' hamster is going to be running the country. This has to stop!

[Here is another mainstream media insert to make up for Moore's stream of consciousness daydreaming on his web site.]

5. The Two Sides Don't Even Talk Anymore
It's worth investigating the yearlong conundrum of why poor, middle-America voters identify so well with an egocentric real estate mogul from New York. "When you say he hasn't read a book in his adult life, you've just described the majority of Americans. Get out of your bubble, everybody!" Moore urged.

[Back to Michael Moore's best stream of consciousness writing]

The Hillary Problem. Can we speak honestly, just among ourselves? And before we do, let me state, I actually like Hillary – a lot – and I think she has been given a bad rap she doesn't deserve. But her vote for the Iraq War made me promise her that I would never vote for her again. To date, I haven't broken that promise. For the sake of preventing a proto-fascist from becoming our commander-in-chief, I'm breaking that promise. I sadly believe Clinton will find a way to get us in some kind of military action. She's a hawk, to the right of Obama. But Trump's psycho finger will be on The Button, and that is that. Done and done.

Let's face it: Our biggest problem here isn't Trump – it's Hillary. She is hugely unpopular — nearly 70% of all voters think she is untrustworthy and dishonest. She represents the old way of politics, not really believing in anything other than what can get you elected. That's why she fights against gays getting married one moment, and the next she's officiating a gay marriage. Young women are among her biggest detractors, which has to hurt considering it's the sacrifices and the battles that Hillary and other women of her generation endured so that this younger generation would never have to be told by the Barbara Bushes of the world that they should just shut up and go bake some cookies. But the kids don't like her, and not a day goes by that a millennial doesn't tell me they aren't voting for her. No Democrat, and certainly no independent, is waking up on November 8th excited to run out and vote for Hillary the way they did the day Obama became president or when Bernie was on the primary ballot. The enthusiasm just isn't there. And because this election is going to come down to just one thing — who drags the most people out of the house and gets them to the polls — Trump right now is in the catbird seat.

The Depressed Sanders Vote. Stop fretting about Bernie's supporters not voting for Clinton – we're voting for Clinton! The polls already show that more Sanders voters will vote for Hillary this year than the number of Hillary primary voters in '08 who then voted for Obama. This is not the problem. The fire alarm that should be going off is that while the average Bernie backer will drag him/herself to the polls that day to somewhat reluctantly vote for Hillary, it will be what's called a "depressed vote" – meaning the voter doesn't bring five people to vote with her. He doesn't volunteer 10 hours in the month leading up to the election. She never talks in an excited voice when asked why she's voting for Hillary. A depressed voter. Because, when you're young, you have zero tolerance for phonies and BS. Returning to the Clinton/Bush era for them is like suddenly having to pay for music, or using MySpace or carrying around one of those big-ass portable phones. They're not going to vote for Trump; some will vote third party, but many will just stay home. Hillary Clinton is going to have to do something to give them a reason to support her — and picking a moderate, bland-o, middle of the road old white guy as her running mate is not the kind of edgy move that tells millennials that their vote is important to Hillary. Having two women on the ticket – that was an exciting idea. But then Hillary got scared and has decided to play it safe. This is just one example of how she is killing the youth vote.

The Jesse Ventura Effect. Finally, do not discount the electorate's ability to be mischievous or underestimate how any millions fancy themselves as closet anarchists once they draw the curtain and are all alone in the voting booth. It's one of the few places left in society where there are no security cameras, no listening devices, no spouses, no kids, no boss, no cops, there's not even a friggin' time limit. You can take as long as you need in there and no one can make you do anything. You can push the button and vote a straight party line, or you can write in Mickey Mouse and Donald Duck. There are no rules. And because of that, and the anger that so many have toward a broken political system, millions are going to vote for Trump not because they agree with him, not because they like his bigotry or ego, but just because they can. Just because it will upset the apple cart and make mommy and daddy mad. And in the same way like when you're standing on the edge of Niagara Falls and your mind wonders for a moment what would that feel like to go over that thing, a lot of people are going to love being in the position of puppetmaster and plunking down for Trump just to see what that might look like. Remember back in the '90s when the people of Minnesota elected a professional wrestler as their governor? They didn't do this because they're stupid or thought that Jesse Ventura was some sort of statesman or political intellectual. They did so just because they could. Minnesota is one of the smartest states in the country. It is also filled with people who have a dark sense of humor — and voting for Ventura was their version of a good practical joke on a sick political system. This is going to happen again with Trump.

Coming back to the hotel after appearing on Bill Maher's Republican Convention special this week on HBO, a man stopped me. "Mike," he said, "we have to vote for Trump. We HAVE to shake things up." That was it. That was enough for him. To "shake things up." President Trump would indeed do just that, and a good chunk of the electorate would like to sit in the bleachers and watch that reality show.

…

Yours,
Michael Moore

Jennifer Harper of the Washington Times in November 2017 reported on the public's reaction to diatribes such as those spewn by Michael Moore. Moore's inarticulate ramblings are representative of an unhinged, unglued constituency, which includes wounded Democrats and a complicit, biased and downright corrupt press.

The public is just not buying it though if you could cull through the garbage Moore writes and speaks you can feel his deep fear from 2016 that Trump would get elected. Ironically, for those of us familiar with the likes of a *hold-your-nose* type of person as Michael Moore, with his fear of Trump projecting to everybody he met, it was far better than a Trump endorsement. It contributed to "Why Trump Got Elected!"

Harper wrote about the relentless, hostile media coverage of President Trump and his administration could be reaching the saturation point. "The public appears weary, wary and quite possibly ready to move on — hungry, perhaps, for credible news coverage over biased caterwaul."

"Unhinged coverage of Trump is hurting the media," wrote Kyle Smith, a columnist for the New York Post who offered his best advice for journalists.

"Turn down the volume. Unclench your fist. Turn the dial back down from 11. Trump isn't going anywhere for a while. Deal with it," Mr. Smith said that while noting that "the lines between news media, lifestyle media and flat-out activism have faded into irrelevance."

Conservative analysts and conservatives in the normal people contingent believe that unprecedented negative coverage of Mr. Trump is actually a symptom of panic in the press, now faced with the president's accomplishments and his unexpected resilience. Trump is surviving and is actually winning.

Journalists cannot handle it as it is like a Saint's fan reliving a thousand times the Minnesota Vikings defeat of the New Orleans Saints in the last ten seconds of a Divisional Playoff game. They simply cannot take losing anymore. Yet, they are too corrupt and in the tank for the Democratic Party that they cannot change their ways

Moore who is known as an American left-wing documentary filmmaker, activist and author, is representative of both the fake news media and the Hollywood elite. The media thinks too much of itself and the more it thinks it can get away with the less it is so.

Their self- adulation of having an important duty in the Trump era is minimized by how they flaunt their disdain for the President as if every day damning Trump is all the news that matters. The people are correct in noticing that the media is filtering everything through an overactive obsessive hatred for Trump that diminishes the few kernels of truth they sometimes are forced to utter.

It is hard to find a good purpose for people like Michael Moore

I suspect God puts us all here for a good reason even if the good reason appears to be a bad reason. I have been a registered Democrat for forty-five years. My dad and I were once proud Democrats but the last pride we shared in voting Democrat was for Bob Casey Sr., a great man and a wonderful governor of Pennsylvania. His son, Bob Jr. IMHO is not worthy of tying the senior Casey's shoes.

Never really thinking that the far-lefties in the new Democrat Party, who care more about illegal aliens than legal, long-time American citizens, would ever again align themselves with my America and an Americans first posture, I have been voting Republican. My dad and I talked it over and we agreed and then we would cast our individual votes.

I was reinforced in the notion that Democrats left me behind a long time ago was when I tried to make sense out of Michael Moore's unintelligible diatribe above. Some people think that his venom is journalism and the Democrat Party Leaders all seem to think Moore's regurgitations are great for business. He sure separates JFK Democrats from riff raff of today. I still hope Democrats can recover but I have no expectations. Reading Michael Moore surely deadens hope for the Party's future. America itself thus has little hope without conservatives really stepping up.

I put the Michael Moore (MM) soliloquy first in this book, so that I could remind the readers of how it is—in the words of what my dad and I would call a lost Democrat. This is not my father's Democratic Party and if it keeps moving left and left and even "lefter." It may not even be a real political party any more.

Whatever happened to Democrats being for the American working man?

Those of us normal Americans, who are Republicans or Democrats, who want the normal people, who are American citizens, to succeed and thrive in America, are not for Michael Moore's values or his distorted vision of America. This means that if you hate American values, you can sign up as a new Michael Moore American. No thank you.

When you have the time, so that this line of thinking stays with you, please go back and read Moore's jeremiad on Trump and his election predictions again. He outdid himself with his rancor. He is surely a better outcome predictor than he is a writer or a sage on the brand of policies that Americans love the most. Go home Michael Moore. If you think you are home, sir. Please relocate towards any of the farthest corners of the earth. Good luck there!

God bless all normal Americans, recognizing that Democrats have lost their legitimate claim to any normalcy. Donald Trump's period as CEO of America is already very fruitful. Check your 401K, please. Remember, a better America, not a Michael Moore America is definitely "Why Trump Got Elected!"

Chapter 2   Trump Was the Only Answer

Love or hate?

You either loved Donald Trump when he ran for President or you hated him. There was no in-between then and there is no in-between now. If you love America, even if you may have trusted Obama, with no good reason, few were not ready for four more Obama years with Hillary Clinton as his new name.

If you never figured that out, or if you are now flirting with the new Winfrey on the block to become the popular president then I regret that you, my friend, are a part of the problem, not the solution. It is a problem that America and Americans must solve before this country can ever be great again.

Can you imagine how successful the anti-American deep state would have been with Mrs. Clinton as president? I thank God, every time I realize that Donald Trump is the President of my United States of America. I can't wait to hear the Oprah's first post-racial address. Since Obama, everything is about race? It is because Democrats have stopped dealing with real American issues such as jobs, and real healthcare for the working class.

After a full year, I still happen to love our President for the right reasons. As I noted in my Chapter 1 editorial, I find him to be a gift from God to the American people in our time of great need.

After all the weak, wimpy, wobbly conservative leaders, groomed by establishment elitism, who offered little recognition or solutions for the concerns of the American citizens; Donald J. Trump, my candidate for president is a deep breath of fresh air.

Thank you, Donald J. Trump for doing the United States a big favor by taking on corruption in both political parties as well as the media. You are doing just fine and my friends and relatives appreciate your taking a hiatus from your wonderful storybook life and using your time to help us. We sure need it.

Though some felt when you ran in 2016 that you were not a viable candidate at the beginning, I was not among their ranks. I saw you grow from day one, when you were introduced to the piranha at the first Republican primary debate. You did very well but nobody would acknowledge you because you were and continue to be the biggest threat to all of the establishment elites in both parties that has ever existed. You are especially not liked by the corrupt press because you call them out on their dishonesty. Thank you, President Trump.

You have taken the Republican electorate by storm and I loved watching you climb higher and higher in the polls, though Hillary C. was always deemed the favorite by the corrupt media. On your way to a great victory, you also won over many Democrats including some in my own family—long time progressives who had enough.

They switched to Republican, so they could vote for you in the PA primary. They are all very smart people, especially my wonderful sister-in-law, Diane who never gave an inch before Trump. She became a Trumpster. It took a while for a lot of Democrats, such as I, to know that today's Democratic leaders are really progressives who care little about the American people and that includes most regular Democrats.

Though the Constitution Party, the Green Party, and the Libertarian Party, and other parties had their own sponsored candidates in the General Election, the importance of this election was well understood by ordinary citizens. Our country was at stake. I expected that many from these parties would vote against the status quo to make America great again. Trump had the only message that resonated with the American people.

I happen to be a lifelong Democrat who is sick of the Democrat Party and the apologetic corrupt anti-American press. At first it seemed unintentional. Now I see it as part of a plan to indoctrinate the American people into believing that socialism and communism and Marxist principles are better than American values. For America to remain strong, the Democrats and Hillary Clinton needed to be defeated. All citizens were needed for us to make this happen and we did.

Congratulations are in order for Donald Trump who is a new guy in a tough political scenario. Despite his lack of funding and lack of support, he was able to overtake all the Republicans, including the whiners and the RINOs and the long-time establishment elites. Trump beat them all. They were ready to take every dollar their donors would give them to buy their support. Trump put up his own bucks and he outsmarted them all and won the biggest deal of his life.

On the way to the win, even Michael Moore said that the Convention really helped the Republicans and the Trump Candidacy, which after a year of Never-Trumpers, must still be tracked separately.

How about that great convention and the first-class rebuttals to the status quo anti-American speeches during Hillary's convention week? It was heartening to see the Republican campaign rubbing a little Trump moxie onto the major coronation that was supposed to take place at the end of July.

The reluctant Hillary endorsement by Bernie Sanders and the Debbie Wasserman Schultz firing showed that the Democrats were the Party of chicanery, deceit, and downright cheating. It is nauseating how far to the dark side of the Force; Democratic leadership has gone. Why can we not, despite all our searching, find an honest Democratic Leader who really loves America.

Was it not a wonderful sight for the Trump family to participate in the convention and the campaign for the good of America? It was a pleasure hearing from Melania, Tiffany, Donald Jr., Eric, and Ivanka. What talent! What a family? Even Ronald Reagan had detractors in his family. Why does Trump's family think he is OK? Maybe because he is!

Please allow a digression for a brief discussion of family talent and how families can do great things together.

My father was one of five Kelly brothers – Ed, Pat, Joe, Mike, & Phil, who were all high-school basketball greats in the 1940's. They played up and down the Wilkes-Barre Wyoming Valley and won their share of many great games against organized teams. Nobody sat on the bench. There were only five Kelly brothers and the bench was always cold.

The Kelly brothers reminded me of the five talent laden Trumps at the convention. It was overwhelming. There was nobody warming the Trump bench because they were all out winning the game—just like the Kelly boys.

As an American worried about America, I am appreciative for the Donald Trump candidacy for lending the Five Trumps to the people of the United States during his ever so important campaign for America. Again, it is both heartwarming and very refreshing. It is just one of many reasons why Trump won the presidency.

We need every one of the Trump soldiers, especially their leader, who thankfully has become our president. There is so much corruption, mostly hate-filled biased media speech that Mr. Trump, Mike Pence, and the whole Trump team could not afford to have anybody out of the contest for too long.

The Trump campaign expected bad stuff to continue--low blows, untruths, unkind assaults, and whatever vile actions the establishment elites, the Democrats, and the corrupt fourth estate choose to unleash. The press chose not to represent America but instead represented the lowest of life's== in the Democratic Party

So, in the final analysis of why Donald Trump won the presidency, it was not because he needed all the Trumps, Mike Pence, the Trump campaign team, and we the people at home to continue the fight against the forces of the dark side. I do not mean to say that was not important. Trump won because he got all the Trumps, Mike Pence, the Trump campaign team, and all of us at home who continued the fight against the forces of the dark side.

Believers did not believe them. Their purpose was deceit. The truth has always been a foreign notion to the Hillary people. When Donald Trump won, all Americans won. My sincere thanks to the Trumps et al for taking on the rot in America to bring America and Americans a big victory.

Too bad we do not have a free press!

The intellectuals of the 18th and 19th centuries, especially Edmund Burke, gave us the notion of Fourth Estate (the press and all other media) as a civil watchdog to keep an eye on those in power. It is very clear from the writing of Thomas Paine and others, who pointed out and also acted upon the idea that we may have just cause to overthrow the state if it is seen to be no longer acting in our interests. This is not trivial. For its own reasons, the press in the US has abdicated its role as the Fourth Estate.

The founders were not thinking "hunting," when they explicitly added the Second Amendment to the Bill of Right. Their reasoning is what really drives Americans to actively defend the second amendment. Though hunting with rifles is important, it is not hunting that is the root cause of the drive by patriotic Americans to protect the founders' intention of second Amendment.

There is the possibility and perhaps there is even a likelihood that sometime in the future, scoundrels would take over the government and would need to be dealt a blow that only an armed citizenry could deliver. The media today from all we can see, would be on the side of the scoundrels so it may not be as easy to defend as the founder's envisioned. Finding the very scoundrels who have been driving our country to perdition to be trying as hard as they can to take our guns away make this notion ever more frightening and real. This is just another of many reasons why Trump was elected.

Today, governments such as ours that make the claim to be acting in the "public interest" must face daily scrutiny of their actions. This is a necessary duty of an alert public in a democratic republic. The government must be called to account when overstepping the bounds of what citizens will support, or when taking actions that are clearly not in our interests.

There was a time when the public could rely on journalists and the news media to do this job on our behalf. This separation between the people and the state becomes more important when the economic interests of the powerful establishment elites so frequently dominate society.

In our modern world, the interest of "the nation," can be deduced to be no more than the collective interest of those who wield political and economic power. That of course in 2016 has gave rise to the silent revolution that put Donald Trump in office. We continue to experience this today as residue of the prior administration operating as the deep state are interfering with a full and clean transition of power. Some worry that the voice of the people has been all but snuffed out by the powerful. The people are mad as hell and are not going to take it anymore. Donald Trump's presidency is proof of that.

Today, the state is the executive branch of the ruling class. And, more and more these "rulers," have stopped believing in a government of the people, by the people, and for the people. Former president Obama claimed to have been a Constitutional Law Professor. Yet he attacked the Constitution daily by taking many unlawful actions of which most are aware.

Remnants of his administration continue their attempts to assault The Constitution, the one document that gives the people all of the rights in America. This is another big reason why Trump got elected. We the people are no longer willing to settle for a government of the government, by the government and for the government. Unfortunately, for eight years before Trump, it would have been difficult to tell.

The news media – as the tribune of "the people" – has a major role as the Fourth Estate to constantly be on guard and alert to actions of the state, particularly when those actions may harm the interests of citizens. In recent years, the Fourth Estate has mostly been absent, serving as a wing of the Democratic Party. Since the onset of the Trump Administration, the fourth estate has actually disappeared. President Trump nonetheless gets his messages out by talking on social media directly to the people. He will do so with or without an honest press.

It would be nice if the press and the corrupt Democratic Party were not joined at the hip today. But for a portion of Fox News and National Radio programs, and of course for the President's Tweets, there would be no truth available in America today. Though the Fourth Estate for over 200 years has been vital to the interests of American citizens, somehow, we are able to do fine without them from Trump's inauguration in 2018.

Because our foes are Donald Trump's foes, while the Trump and Pence campaign gained momentum before its victory in November 2016, emboldened Trump haters on both sides of the political spectrum – the Bush supporters and Clinton Supporters, got more vicious. In response, the people of America, aligned with the values brought forth in the Trump campaign fought back because there simply was no room to lose this battle against the dark forces, who for their own selfish interests were determined to keep the country weak. And so, we have yet another reason for the Trump victory.

From the moment the TEA Party was born, and even now that the TEA is not as visible, Americans have been unwilling to take it anymore. While wishing and hoping that the establishment would find its way and begin to represent the people in the way that got them elected, Donald Trump gave us a true hope that we could do it without the establishment.

Trump helped Americans once again feel that America is God's Country or as President Reagan would call it, *a Shining City upon a Hill*. The times from the recent past when there were glimmers from empty promises that were never fulfilled are over. Americans demanded and got a responsive government as promised by Donald Trump and Mike Pence. Yes, this too is a big reason why Trump got elected.

It is the reason why so many of us joined with Donald Trump and the Trump family and the Trump campaign to get rid of the wretched establishment swamp. With Trump's clear and refreshing messages about making America great again, we became his loyal supporters. We elected Trump because we trust him.

We continue to believe that Donald Trump will keep his word as have presidents of the past such as John Fitzgerald Kennedy and Ronald Wilson Reagan. I can still see the Five Trumps playing on the first team at the convention, all believing in the Trump candidacy and in America and Americans. When it was America's turn to believe in the whole Trump family, we elected Donald J. Trump as our president. We are still smiling.

We the people have simply gotten sick of everything for the Republican big shots. We tired of the establishment elites such as the George Bushes, Jeb Bush, Carl Rove, Britt Hume, the US Chamber of Commerce, and the many donors who think they can buy America simply by buying its weak, whiny, and wimpy politicians.

Meanwhile we see the Democrats of today brewing up one falsehood after another for the corrupt press to spread on an unwary accepting public. Their objective right from the beginning has been to finish off the Trump team by telling enough lies that the people would finally believe them and acquiesce.

This will not happen this time! Democrat constituents saw the vile of the dishonest Democratic Party leaders and Hillary Clinton when they destroyed Bernie Sanders in a conspiracy of lies and double-dealing. More and more Democrats left the Party to vote for Donald Trump in primaries across the country and then, they stuck with Trump as the only salvation for the country right through the general election to today. That's why Trump got elected.

A small establishment elite had been running the Republican Party for far too long. They rigged the game against the people and were accustomed to things going their way. The beauty of the Trump election was that these RINOs got caught flat-footed when their old tricks and their "ram it quietly down their throats," tactics simply did not work this time.

Why? It was because Donald Trump, the antitheses of the establishment had already entered the arena, and he proceeded to knock the elites over one by one. Along the way he convinced the majority of Americans in a majority of the states that he was the real deal. And, so, we elected him President. The Trump honesty continues to be refreshing despite him being under attack by the most dishonest political class in US history.

The rise of Trump was nothing less than a tidal wave. In their deluded minds, the establishment actually thought they could steal the nomination from Donald Trump and that their strategy would work just the same as it did against Ron Paul in 2012. But Trump has a constituency, which includes you and yours truly. that would not stand for it. And, so, he got elected in 2016 as a people's favorite.

I am reminded of Japanese Naval Marshal General Isoroku Yamamoto who, after Pearl Harbor confessed: "I fear all we have done is to awaken a sleeping giant and filled him with a terrible resolve." The attempts of the establishment elites to derail the Trump Campaign were thwarted by a fed-up public. We wanted Trump, period! We the public had gotten very sick of Republican broken promises. We lost trust in the Party elite leaders and the donors who no longer care about the people. And, with firm resolve we won the presidential election for Donald Trump.

Yes, Donald Trump did manage to awaken the silent majority of Americans who previously either did not care or simply did not bother to vote. Some in the past just shrugged their shoulders and accepted that the system was rigged and that all of the little men in the world—all of us insignificant citizens of America, could not make an impact under any circumstances. Trump is the difference. The people rose up and are taking our power back. That is Trump got elected.

Today, despite the dirty Democrats creating falsehoods to take him down, Donald J. Trump has become a leader for the non-elites. John Casick, Marco Rubio, Mitt Romney, John McCain, all the Bushes and even one-time stalwarts on Fox News such as George Will and Charles Krauthammer, and Brit Hume are viewed to be on the wrong side of history by we Americans who won the election for Donald J. Trump. I turn the channel when I see them. I listen to radio greats Laura Ingraham, Sean Hannity, Michael Savage, and Rush Limbaugh and their truth satisfies my need for the real news of today.

Trump has always been for the non-establishment brand of citizen, who simply depends on honest representatives to keep our democratic republic operating smoothly. He is the perfect alternative to candidates who do the bidding of Bush's and Clintons and their ilk, who somehow have become richer and richer while the ordinary people have become poorer and poorer. Donald J. Trump became the perfect alternative for leaders who had permitted America herself to be turned into a debt-ridden shadow of its once great self.

Unfortunately, because of elitist propaganda from both Republicans and Democrat members of the establishment, in full cahoots with the corrupt main stream media, the fourth estate, full of journalists that have forgotten American History, Americans chose a quiet revolt. We hear it all and are disgusted and we are lined up against those still willing and eager to put forth their hatred against Donald Trump like as if it is the common opinion. We voted for Donald Trump against all those lies and the daily soap opera.

Unfortunately, because there were some voters who do not have a high information threshold, I felt compelled to write a book titled, 101 Secrets How to be a High Information Voter. This was to help serve as an antidote to the misinformation and lies of the establishment on both sides of the aisle.

The Democrats and the Bushes nonetheless continued to promote their negative message through the corrupt, dishonest press. Some low information voters accepted the bias towards then candidate Donald Trump and now accept it against President Trump as if it were true. It is not. That is why I wrote this book. *Why Trump Got Elected?* Donald Trump's supporters including cross-over Democrats would elect him today even if he ran against the Oprah. Mr. Trump, after just one year is well on his way to being one of America's best presidents ever.

Because of the many of us who had been inundated with negative Trump messages every day, who found it difficult to find the truth in the mainstream news, we Trump supporters chose not to be quiet when we are in a group. We speak up and let the chips fall where they may. I have lost a few friends who demanded that I never mention Trump's name in their company? There is nothing I can do about that but pray that one day, they will soften as the truth comes in.

Despite some adversity, like apostles and good disciples of a great message to save America, we, who actually saw the light early on, had no choice but to refute the lies that were circulating every day. The ham-handed efforts of the Soros crowd to smear Mr. Trump as a racist were shown to be the lies that they are. That's why Trump got elected.

There is great irony in the notion of racism today and Republicans, who have the winning hand, fail to talk about it and so since it is not taught truthfully in the schools nobody knows about the Democrats and their racist history. What has been happening in recent times is that with a complicit press, Democrats are rewriting history and will claim that Donald Trump is racist if he mentions anything they can grab on to such as the color of a wall.

The truth is that Al Gore's dad and Bill Clinton and many other prominent profiles in Democratic Politics, especially those from the South, such as Arkansas lie about the Democratic role in the idea of slavery and the idea of blacks having equal rights. Yet, the black leaders let the Democrats get away with it.

Reframing of the relevant history is the story of the Democratic party in a nutshell. The party's history is pockmarked with racism and terror. It was the Democrats, and not the Republicans who were the party of slavery. They were for black codes, Jim Crow, and that miserable terrorist excrescence, the Ku Klux Klan. All White people are not Republicans.

Republicans were the party of Lincoln, Reconstruction, anti-lynching laws, and the civil rights acts of 1875, 1957, 1960, and 1964. It was not the slippery lying Democrats. Of course, not all Republicans were models of rectitude on racial matters? However, a light look at a few pages of history and you would find that Republicans were a heck of a lot better than the Democrats? Without question.

As recently as 2010, the Senate's president pro tempore was former Ku Klux Klan Exalted Cyclops Robert Byrd (D., W.Va.). Rather than acknowledge their sorry history, modern Democrats choose to rewrite it or simply lie about. Today, in fact just today, Donald J. Trump is a racist again because Democrats have said so. He supposedly said that destitute places like Haiti are hellholes to live in.

Democrats say this all the time as they seek aid for Haitians. Trump is reported to have used a different four-letter word and he supposedly mentioned Norway as a nice place from which we might look for immigrants if we are surveying the world for the best people.

Rand Paul, interviewed on Fox on January 15, 2018, noted that he was getting serious threats on social media because he told the truth about Trump, before he ran for President, being one of the champions of Haiti when the Doctor / Senator needed funding to conduct cataract operations in Haiti. Fund put up a ton of money for the Haitians and about 200 or so, who could not see at all were given the gift of sight.

Has anybody seen that on the fake news channels? Has any Democrat matched that level of beneficence and munificence? What gives Democrats and the corrupt press the right to pick the racists when their own records are as noted—"pockmarked with racism and terror."

With the press and the Democrats being habitual liars, trying to damn and destroy anything in their political paths, we can surely say that is "Why Trump Got Elected.!" The truth is mighty and refreshing.

Many of our neighbors found it increasingly difficult to acknowledge that the democratic foundation of our nation as well as American sovereignty was being destroyed by the very people who had been conspiring to stop Trump's nomination. They were giving up our America and easing us towards their socialist / communist New World Order.

We who pay attention, even today with powerful forces at work trying to impeach our duly elected president, must continue to be alert and we must be prepared for the assault. We must keep speaking up and doing better in helping our friends and neighbors see through the media lies and the lies of the Democratic leadership. The Democrats of today would be against Superman, whose mission was "truth, justice, and the American way!

We are making progress for sure as people who would never even use the word Republican in public, have done the unthinkable. They have even changed parties, so they could vote for Trump in the primary and then they followed through in the general election. From my observations, they are still at it. We and they are "Why Trump Got Elected!"

Chapter 3 The US Needs Donald Trump?

A billionaire who captured the admiration of the people.

I secretly smiled whenever I thought about the prospects of Donald J. Trump becoming the 45th President of the United States of America. I smiled each time I wrote about it actually happening and I am still smiling. I also smile about it in public but sometimes that does get me in trouble.

Again in 2017/2018, my party, the Democratic Party has abandoned the working class and it is now the party of the fringe. I am not on the fringe. The Party of the fringe had a leader on the fringe for eight years he set my country back so far that it is taking a strong man like Donald Trump longer than it should to bring America back. Donald Trump is the solution. As many have said before me, Hillary Clinton would have been Obama's third term.

Democrats would deny the poor and the middle class a tax break just to that Donald Trump does not get any positive press. Are they schlocks or what? The Senate tax bill is already reducing income taxes for people at every income level--even those who don't pay taxes. That's the official conclusion of the Joint Committee on Taxation. Check it out. But, Democrats of today would rather lie than give their own people a break. What a shame.

Can a person be black and conservative?

Who gets to decide? Every solution is intended to address a problem. Barack Hussein Obama and the prospects of a third term via Hillary was seen as a big, big problem by Americans who spend 2/3 of their day awake. That's "Why Trump Got Elected!" The Trump presidency is already solving big Obama era problems.

I received this email unexpectedly in 2016. It is about a note that black conservative writer Sylvia Thompson wrote about our former president's legacy and what he has done to us to achieve it. With Democrats playing identity politics every day, I wanted to correctly identify Ms. Thompson. What a great mind!

Sylvia Thompson knows Barack Obama

I looked this email up on Snopes but did not find it. However, I found Sylvia's web site link, so I have provided the full link to her site, so you can enjoy more of her work. Thank you, Sylvia.

http://www.renewamerica.com/columns/sthompson/151026

Here is the email:

It begins with a quote from an unknown person in the email chain

"She is "right on". I have been saying Impeach Him [Obama] or the last year."

Subject: Sylvia Thompson WOW

Sylvia Thompson on Obama's "legacy".

Sylvia Thompson is a black conservative writer whose aim is to counter the liberal spin on issues pertaining to race and culture. Ms. Thompson is a copy editor by trade currently residing in Tennessee

Sylvia Thompson on Obama's "legacy"

THIS IS WHAT SHE HAD TO SAY:

To the many gullible souls out there who truly think that Barack Hussein Obama is "legacy building" in his all-out assault on America, I implore you to bow out of the conversation because you are not seeing clearly.

The term legacy carries positive connotations of something bequeath that is to the receiver's benefit. Everything that Barack Hussein Obama does is calculated to destroy America, which he despises. This man no more cares about legacy than he fears being properly prosecuted by the white political leaders whose responsibility it is to remove him from office.

I focus on white leaders, because whites are still in the majority and they fill the majority of political offices. If the majority of political operatives were of some other ethnicity, I would lodge my complaint against that group. Ethnicity is an issue only because Obama is half-black, and he uses that fact to intimidate guilt-conflicted white people. Otherwise, he would have been impeached and likely in prison for treason by now.

Barack Hussein Obama's sole aim has been, since he first entered politics and continues as he winds down this presidency, the complete destruction of America as it was founded.

It is an insult to the intelligence of all Americans who must listen to elitist pundits on Fox news and elsewhere, and political drones in either party endeavor to make Obama's behavior fit a pattern of normalcy. Attributing his destructive policies to "legacy building" is either self-delusion on the part of the people who make that claim or cowardliness.

This is my take.

Obama's nuclear deal with Iran has nothing to do with legacy but rather to enable a Muslim nation to wage nuclear war with America and Israel-- the two nations that he most despises.

Does anyone wonder why Russians praise Vladimir Putin despite what the rest of the world might think of him? Putin cares about his country, that's why.

Obama despises the American military because traditionally it has been a mainstay of America's strength, and our strength infuriates him. [Both Obama and Hillary are disciples of Rules for Radicals author and radical Saul Alinsky. Hillary is the greatest Alinsky fan living today as she met the author and was also a great friend.]

Imposition of a polluting homosexual, anti-Christian agenda upon the military ranks destroys unit cohesion and literally terrorizes male members with the prospect of sodomy rape. Such rapes have increased since the forcing of open homosexuality in the ranks, against the will of a majority of members I might add. Couple that with an infiltration of women, for whom all standards of strength must be reduced, and Obama attains his goal of emasculating and demoralizing the forces.

He could not care less about a legacy of making the forces more diverse. Besides, President Truman diversified the military as much as it should be when he integrated it. Obama's objective is its destruction.

Obama reopened relations with Cuba because Cuba is Communist. Legacy is not his concern here either, but rather to scuttle America's attempts to keep Communist influence out of the Americas. That Cuba has major issues with human rights does not matter. Like his Marxist African father before him, he despises the West and all that it represents.

Obama lawlessly declares open borders and amnesty for illegal aliens, because he wants to overrun America with third-world people who bring little more than dependency with them. This tactic not only does not ensure a legacy, but rather it guarantees the eventual conversion of America itself into third-world status, if it is allowed to continue.

Bill Clinton started the travesty of increasing the numbers of third-world immigrants at the expense of culturally more suited immigrants from European and European-influenced nations, but Obama has taken the trend to lawless, destructive extremes. He is fully aware that many of these invaders have no intention of assimilating.

It is only the outcry of a majority of Americans that holds back this hateful invasion scheme, and Donald Trump's entry onto the political scene to oppose that scheme is a saving grace for our nation.

These are but a few instances of behavior that display the loathsome character of Barack Hussein Obama. And he is allowed to roam freely through the American landscape poisoning and polluting as he goes, sure in the realization that no one will stop him because he is "black."

The day that we no longer have to hear the prattle about his "legacy building" will not be soon enough for me.

Many, many Americans are thoroughly fed up with Barack Obama and the spineless crop of political leaders who ignore his criminality. It is yet unknown whether Republicans will ever garner the backbone to become a true opposition party and hold him accountable. Promising signs are the House conservatives' getting rid of establishment types John Boehner and Kevin McCarthy as House Speaker and Speaker hopeful, respectively, and Donald Trump's entry into the 2016 presidential race with enough money and testicular fortitude to tell the Establishment and the Left where to shove it.

Should these positive trends not continue, and the 2016 election cycle yield no movement to counter all the harm that Barack Obama has done to this nation, I think there will be massive disruption. Those folks in the National Rifle Association ads currently running on television seem very serious to me, and that is a good thing.

--- end-of email ---

Chapter 4 Was Hillary a Good Candidate?

The pundits all have an opinion

Many pundits have armchair quarterbacked the 2016 election and many have openly noted that Mrs. Clinton was not the best candidate that the Democrats could have run. Former Vice President Joe Biden has his own opinion and it mirrors those of the pundits. He is still being quoted about Hillary Clinton and the 2016 election. Some think that is why Joe has yet to refuse to rule out running again for president in 2020.

In an interview at a hedge fund conference in Las Vegas in mid-2017, he was asked about Hillary and he had no problem squaring off: Biden said this of Clinton: "I never thought she was a great candidate. I thought I was a great candidate." Well, how about that.

I received a Hillary and Trump email

Sometimes when writing, figuring out how to get the essence of one's message out on the table, it takes a lot of thought. In a book describing why Trump got elected, I felt that it would be to discussed Donald Trump as the anti-Obama and that I could let most of my gems on Hillary in my desk.

After living eight years with a former president who acted like America was a land of guano, and Americans were the ones producing the guano, my intention when I began this chapter was to highlight Trump as the answer to Obama. That is "Why Trump Got elected!"

Other than being a continuation of the Obama administration, I did not think that I had to highlight specific reasons for why Hillary's policies or her past were needed for people to reject her and choose Trump. Then, I got this email and I knew I had to include it in this book.

I received it after I had basically finished the outline and the first draft of this book. It was intended to be serious, thought provoking and somewhat funny and it is all of those plus it also sheds additional light on why Trump got elected.

The scenario depicted is a bar in which Hillary and Trump are having a conversation and they are trying to determine which scandal it was, in which the media were really tearing Hillary apart.

Enjoy. I know Trump supporters will get the message. Following this email, this chapter will end.

X-Virus-Scanned: Debian amavisd-new at dhcp-135.mgmt.ptd.net
Sun, 31 Jul 2016 06:58:13 -0700 (PDT)
Date: Sun, 31 Jul 2016 13:55:23 +0000 (UTC)
From: "Rita Eniorita"

Subject: Interesting

Donald Trump and Hillary Clinton are in a bar. Donald leans over, and with a smile on his face, says,

"The media are really tearing you apart for That Scandal."

Hillary: "You mean my lying about Benghazi?"
Trump: "No, the other one."

Hillary: "You mean the massive voter fraud?"
Trump: "No, the other one."

Hillary: "You mean the military not getting their votes counted?"
Trump: "No, the other one."

Hillary: "Using my secret private server with classified material to Hide my Activities?"
Trump: "No, the other one."

Hillary: "The NSA monitoring our phone calls, emails and everything Else?"
Trump: "No, the other one."

Hillary: "Using the Clinton Foundation as a cover for tax evasion, hiring cronies, and taking bribes from foreign countries?
Trump: "No, the other one."

Hillary: "You mean the drones being operated in our own country without The Benefit of the law?"
Trump: "No, the other one."

Hillary: "Giving 123 Technologies $300 Million, and right afterward it Declared Bankruptcy and was sold to the Chinese?"
Trump: "No, the other one."

Hillary: "You mean arming the Muslim Brotherhood and hiring them in the White House?"
Trump: "No, the other one."

Hillary: "Whitewater, Watergate committee, Vince Foster, commodity Deals?"
Trump: "No the other one:"

Hillary: "The IRS targeting conservatives?"
Trump: "No the other one:"

Hillary: "Turning Libya into chaos?"
Trump: "No the other one:"

Hillary: "Trashing Mubarak, one of our few Muslim friends?"
Trump: "No the other one:"

Hillary: "Turning our backs on Israel?"
Trump: "No the other one:"

Hillary: "The joke Iran Nuke deal? "
Trump: "No the other one:"

Hillary: "Leaving Iraq in chaos? "
Trump: "No, the other one."

Hillary: "The DOJ spying on the press?"
Trump: "No, the other one."

Hillary: "You mean former HHS Secretary Sibelius shaking down health insurance Executives?"
Trump: "No, the other one."

Hillary: "Giving our cronies in SOLYNDRA $500 MILLION DOLLARS and 3 Months Later they declared bankruptcy and then the Chinese bought it?"
Trump: "No, the other one."

Hillary: "The NSA monitoring citizens' ?"
Trump: "No, the other one."

Hillary: "The State Department interfering with an Inspector General Investigation on departmental sexual misconduct?"
Trump: "No, the other one."

Hillary: "Me, The IRS, Clapper and Holder all lying to Congress?"
Trump: "No, the other one."

Hillary: "Threats to all of Bill's former mistresses to keep them quiet"
Trump: "No, the other one."

Hillary: "You mean taking the $145,000,000.00 from Putin for the Uranium Bribe?"
Trump: "No the other one."

Hillary: "I give up! ... Oh wait, I think I've got it! When I stole the White House furniture, silverware and China when Bill left Office?"

Trump: "THAT'S IT! I almost forgot about that one".

****
Everything above is true. Yet she still got a ton of Democratic votes. It causes one to ask, Could there be that uninformed people in this country? D

-- End-of received email --

And that is Why Trump Got Elected!

Chapter 5 What is Donald Trump?

Right or wrong about Trump?

I have such a wonderful group of email friends that I never feel alone. Over the years, we of like mind have gotten to know each other well so that rather than just ideological arguments which go no place, we send each other emails that help substantiate the conservative position. I, of course am a conservative Democrat like JFK, and more than likely I am the only Democrat on the email list.

If you, like me are a Trump guy, even if you cannot come up with a catch-phrase to tell it all in a quick sound bite, think of this next email as a continuous sound bite designed to tell us all we need about *What is a Donald Trump.*

Like other emails that I have used to help us all know "Why Trump Got Elected!" this one is right on the mark. I did not write any of this email unless it is a comment in brackets []. It was sent early in 2016. With people thinking like this, it is easier to see how Trump pulled off his great victory. I hope you like it. It is just what the doctor ordered:

Sent: 1/28/2016 10:06:38 A.M. Eastern Standard Time
Subj: OMG- a 'Keeper'- "What Is Donald Trump?" (So well written & FUNNY too!)

I did a search on 'truthorfiction.com' (I don't trust Snopes.) for the author Don Frederick & there's one by that name who writes for Bloomberg, but I could not find this particular column. --- It's great, whether he wrote it or not.

The author (Don Frederick) is the political correspondent for Bloomberg and he wrote extensively about Obama even before he was elected, and he did it with facts and more facts.

Here goes:

"Who is Donald Trump?" The better question may be, "What is Donald Trump?"

The answer: A giant middle finger from average Americans to the political and media establishment.

Some Trump supporters are like the 60s white girls who dated black guys just to annoy their parents. But most Trump supporters have simply had it with the Demosocialists and the "Republicans in Name Only."

They know there isn't a dime's worth of difference between Hillary Rodham and Jeb Bush, and only a few cents worth between Rodham and the other GOP candidates.

Ben Carson is not an "establishment" candidate, but the Clinton machine would pulverize Carson, and the somewhat rebellious Ted Cruz will (justifiably so) be tied up with natural born citizen lawsuits (as might Marco Rubio).

The Trump supporters figure they may as well have some fun tossing Molotov cocktails at Wall Street and Georgetown while they watch the nation collapse. Besides, lightning might strike, Trump might get elected, and he might actually fix a few things. Stranger things have happened. (The nation elected a Marxist in 2008 and Bruce Jenner now wears designer dresses.)

Millions of conservatives are justifiably furious. They gave the Republicans control of the House in 2010 and control of the Senate in 2014 and have seen them govern no differently than Nancy Pelosi and Harry Reid. Yet those same voters are supposed to trust the GOP in 2016? Why? Trump did not come from out of nowhere. His candidacy was created by the last six years of Republican failures.

No reasonable person can believe that any of the establishment candidates will slash federal spending, rein in the Federal Reserve, cut burdensome business regulations, reform the tax code, or eliminate useless federal departments (the Departments of Education, Housing and Urban Development, Energy, etc.). Even Ronald Reagan was unable to eliminate the Department of Education. (Of course, getting shot at tends to make a person less of a risk-taker.)

No reasonable person can believe that any of the nation's major problems will be solved by Rodham, Bush, and the other dishers of donkey fazoo now eagerly eating corn in Iowa and pancakes in New Hampshire.

Many Americans, and especially Trump supporters, have had it with:

- ✓ Anyone named Bush
- ✓ Anyone named Clinton
- ✓ Anyone who's held political office
- ✓ Political correctness
- ✓ Illegal immigration
- ✓ Massive unemployment
- ✓ Phony "official" unemployment and inflation figures
- ✓ Welfare waste and fraud
- ✓ People faking disabilities to go on the dole
- ✓ VA waiting lists
- ✓ TSA airport groping
- ✓ ObamaCare
- ✓ The Federal Reserve's money-printing schemes
- ✓ Wall Street crooks like Jon Corzine
- ✓ Michelle Obama's vacations
- ✓ Michelle Obama's food police
- ✓ Barack Obama's golf
- ✓ Barack Obama's arrogant and condescending lectures
- ✓ Barack Obama's criticism/hatred of America
- ✓ Valerie Jarrett
- ✓ "Holiday trees"
- ✓ Hollywood hypocrites
- ✓ Global warming nonsense
- ✓ Cop killers

- ✓ Gun confiscation threats
- ✓ Stagnant wages
- ✓ Chevy Volts
- ✓ Clock boy
- ✓ Pajama boy
- ✓ Mattress girl
- ✓ Boys in girls' bathrooms
- ✓ Whiny, spoiled college students who can't even place the Civil War in the correct century

...and that's just the short list.

Trump supporters believe that no Democrat wants to address these issues, and that few Republicans have the courage to address these issues. They certainly know that none of the establishment candidates are better than barely listening to them, and Trump is their way of saying, "Screw you, Hillary Rodham Rove Bush!"

The more the talking head political pundits insult the Trump supporters, the more supporters he gains. (The only pundits who seem to understand what is going on are Democrats Doug Schoen and Pat Caddell and Republican John LeBoutillier. All the others argue that the voters will eventually "come to their senses" and support an establishment candidate.)

But America does not need a tune-up at the same old garage. It needs a new engine installed by experts--and neither Rodham nor Bush are mechanics with the skills or experience to install it. Hillary Rodham is not a mechanic; she merely manages a garage her philandering husband abandoned. Jeb Bush is not a mechanic; he merely inherited a garage. Granted, Trump is also not a mechanic, but he knows where to find the best ones to work in his garage. He won't hire his brother-in-law or someone to whom he owes a favor; he will hire someone who lives and breathes cars.

"How dare they revolt!" the "elites" are bellowing. Well, the citizens are daring to revolt, and the RINOs had better get used to it. "But Trump will hand the election to Clinton!" That is what the Karl Rove-types want people to believe, just as the leftist media eagerly shoved "Maverick" McCain down GOP throats in 2008--knowing he would lose to Obama.

But even if Trump loses and Rodham wins, she would not be dramatically different than Bush or most of his fellow candidates. They would be nothing more than caretakers, not working to restore America's greatness but merely presiding over the collapse of a massively in-debt nation. A nation can perhaps survive open borders; a nation can perhaps survive a generous welfare system. But no nation can survive both--and there is little evidence that the establishment candidates of either party understand that. The United States cannot forever continue on the path it is on. At some point it will be destroyed by its debt.

Yes, Trump speaks like a bull wandering through a china shop, but the truth is that the borders do need to be sealed; we cannot afford to feed, house, and clothe 200,000 Syrian immigrants for decades (even if we get inordinately lucky and none of them are ISIS infiltrators or Syed Farook wannabes); the world is at war with radical Islamists; all the world's glaciers are not melting; and Rosie O'Donnell is a fat pig.

Is Trump the perfect candidate? Of course not. Neither was Ronald Reagan. But unless we close our borders and restrict immigration, all the other issues are irrelevant. One terrorist blowing up a bridge or a tunnel could kill thousands. One jihadist poisoning a city's water supply could kill tens of thousands. One electromagnetic pulse attack from a single Iranian nuclear device could kill tens of millions. Faced with those possibilities, most Americans probably don't care that Trump relied on eminent domain to grab up a final quarter acre of property for a hotel, or that he boils the blood of the Muslim Brotherhood thugs running the Council on American-Islamic Relations.

While Attorney General Loretta Lynch's greatest fear is someone giving a Muslim a dirty look, most Americans are more worried about being gunned down at a shopping mall by a crazed lunatic who treats his prayer mat better than his three wives and who thinks 72 virgins are waiting for him in paradise.

The establishment is frightened to death that Trump will win, but not because they believe he will harm the nation. They are afraid he will upset their taxpayer-subsidized apple carts. While Obama threatens to veto legislation that spends too little, they worry that Trump will veto legislation that spends too much.

You can be certain that if an establishment candidate wins in November 2016, his or her cabinet positions will be filled with the same people we've seen before. The washed-up has-beens of the Clinton and Bush administrations will be back in charge. The hacks from Goldman Sachs will continue to call the shots. Whether it is Bush's Karl Rove or Clinton's John Podesta who makes the decisions in the White House will matter little. If the establishment wins, America loses.

Don Fredrick   December 10, 2015

-- End of email --

Chapter 6 Trump and Immigration

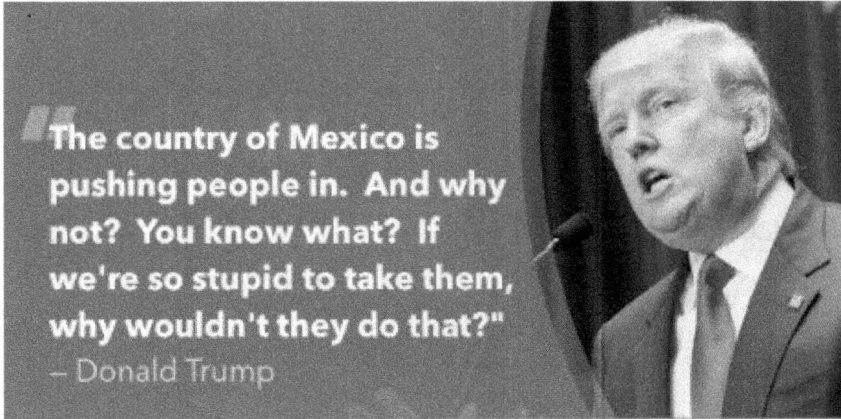

"The country of Mexico is pushing people in. And why not? You know what? If we're so stupid to take them, why wouldn't they do that?"
— Donald Trump

Concerns and Solutions

Moving to the immigration front and leaving the prior email behind for us all to chew upon some more, let's finish this chapter by squeezing in a few items regarding immigration in bullet form and then a little text. You have seen all these notions but perhaps not all together at once. This is the immigration issue in a nutshell followed by the solution for the 60 million foreign interlopers in the US today.

Trump gets it. And that alone on immigration is enough reason "Why Trump Got Elected!"

What do Americans want?

- ✓ No amnesty
- ✓ No citizenship
- ✓ No voting ever!
- ✓ Jobs first for Americans!
- ✓ No employer cost advantage for hiring interlopers
- ✓ No freebies? No free rides for illegal foreigners
- ✓ Mandatory registration -- no shadows -- we must know who they are

- ✓ Americans get all the breaks
- ✓ No more misguided love"
- ✓ Eliminate need for terms illegal and undocumented
- ✓ No need for DACA or sanctuary cities
- ✓ Programs that pay for themselves
- ✓ Interlopers from other countries pay back all benefits
- ✓ Solution for anchor citizens

What do interlopers want?

- ✓ A nice safe place to live
- ✓ No fear and no hiding
- ✓ No more shadow living
- ✓ Opportunity to have a job
- ✓ Opportunity to keep jobs held
- ✓ No wage less than minimum wage
- ✓ A life without persecution or danger

Few think this problem is solvable: I do! I created the Pay-to-Go Plan and the Resident Visa Plan, both of which are described in detail in books of the same name.

Before I wrote the Resident Visa Plan and the Pay-to-Go plan books a few years ago. this book, called the Lifetime Guest Plan, contained most of the precepts necessary to solve the problem of 60 million interlopers in America.

The Resident Visa Plan

- ✓ Stern and sane, pro-American
- ✓ Compassionate plan
- ✓ Serves both citizens and interlopers alike
- ✓ No more shadows
- ✓ No fear and no hiding
- ✓ Americans are no longer last
- ✓ Americans no longer pick up the tab

The US has 60 million interlopers in residence

- ✓ From around the world.
- ✓ Not necessarily bad people.
- ✓ Take US education & healthcare & never give back
- ✓ Take US jobs – work cheap
- ✓ Taxpayers pay for Congress's munificence
- ✓ Republicans & US business: want cheap wages
- ✓ Democrats: want new Dem voters
- ✓ Congress does nothing; POTUS--BHO made it worse
- ✓ If Congress wanted a cheap solution: Cost of Resident Visa Program is zero
- ✓ Program turns worthy dependent illegal foreign nationals into paying lifetime guests.
- ✓ Those not granted guest status registration are deported. No country would want them.
- ✓ Guests don't have any intrinsic US rights
- ✓ They get only specific privileges as granted by citizens.
- ✓ Resident Visa Holders must always behave well.

"A guest is a person who is invited to visit the home or office or country or take part in a function organized by another."

This plan was built for the 60 million interlopers already in America; not designed to permit future interlopers. Why do we have 60 million interlopers in the US today?

FYI: An interloper is a person who becomes involved in a place or situation where they are not wanted or are considered not to belong. Interloper is not a synonym for undocumented immigrant, but most illegal aliens can rightfully be called interlopers. Another way of saying this is that Interlopers are uninvited guests.

My message about interlopers is not one of guilt for Americans but it is one that hopefully will help those who know they are interlopers to get on the right track. It is time to begin to love America and do what is necessary to get on the right side of American law.

No more shadows; No more freebies; No more costs for Taxpayers

Can a Trump plan help Americans?

✓ Plan must register all interlopers.
✓ All applicants get vetted.
✓ Appeal may be initiated by registrant or US official
✓ Aspirant provides address and demographics
✓ Fingerprints, retina scans etc.
✓ $200 first time; $100 annual fee for renewal

Immigration is not the only issue that helped Trump get elected.
However, it was very big in Americans choosing Trump over those
who were OK stiffing America and Americans.

Chapter 7 Trump Worked Hard to Become President

Wants to be best president ever

I waited a little bit, until this chapter, before I told you in Donald John Trump's words Why Trump Got Elected. It is no secret. Trump got elected because he is Trump. Nobody else could have pulled it off. Nobody else! He told us he would be our next president and like many others, I believed him. Seventeen Republicans and four Democrats for sure did not believe him. The low information crowd in America did not believe him either but then again, they got all their information from the Democratic Party and the low-ratings, corrupt, fake-news media. Most never heard the truth once during the one and a half-year campaign for office.

Yet, Trump told us all, believers and non-believers that he would be our next president, how he would become our president, and why he would be our next president. He told it to us all on June 16, 2015, and he did not waiver off point for over a year and a half. Then he walked away with the presidency despite the polls and despite the lies of Democratic leaders who are still shell-shocked.

Trump struck a chord with the American people. The Obama administration was one lie after another. Eventually all these little time bombs went off and those of us paying attention knew we needed something big to get America back on track. Donald Trump supersized his campaign and he promised to supersize America when elected. He promised quite simply to Make America Great Again. His message said it all. It was clear and energizing and it made Americans feel good that somebody who cared was finally going to run America.

You can take any of Trump's 186 primary rallies or his 137 general election rallies across the United States and his message was the same as it was on June 16, 2015 when he walked down the elevator at Trump Towers with Melania to get in the presidential foray. Make America Great Again with facts and plans to match.

Big crowds always turned out to support Trump, but Team Clinton didn't get the picture. Disaffected Democrats who felt isolated from their own party and fed up with gridlock did march to the polls, but they did not march to Hillary's few major rallies. They were tired of the way things worked or did not work so they joined Republicans who found Trump distasteful but preferable to Clinton. They wanted help, not hope. My two sisters-in-law, who had always been stalwart Democrats before 2016, joined their ranks; so, I knew the movement to Trump was very real.

In all fairness, Hillary Clinton was out on the trail a lot herself but mostly in the primary season and mostly for functional / organizational meetings and fundraisers. Hillary had learned the art of speaking through the years and she got a lot of practice before she officially threw her hat in the ring.

For example, between April 2013 and March 2015, she gave 91 paid speeches averaging $235,304.35 apiece, for a total of $21,648,000. Three weeks after delivering the last speech, on April 12, 2015, she entered the race.

As long as there was a nice check available, Clinton would speak to just about anyone who was willing to pay the toll, including a scrap metal and recycling conference in Las Vegas, the automobile dealer's association in New Orleans and the National Association of Convenience Stores in Atlanta.

She was called on her exorbitant speaking fees on a number of occasions, but she argued that her fees from speeches at universities went to the Clinton Foundation and not directly into her pocket. Despite the apparent assurances, students at the University of Nevada Las Vegas protested her $225,000 payload as the university was hiking their tuition.

When she entered the race for the primary, she was very active on the trail, but she was not as active and alive as the general election progressed. She did have rallies but not many and they were not big. Donald Trump noticed and commented: "I have to say, we have rallies like this and we have seven, eight, nine, ten thousand routinely," he boasted back in September at a stop in North Carolina. "Hillary goes out for rallies and yesterday I think she had 200 people, maybe 300." That's Why Trump Got Elected.

Wikipedia did a fine job of capturing all the Trump rallies and the attendance. Before we look at Trump's kickoff speech in the next chapter from right after he came down the escalator at Trump Towers, check out this table. It shows all the energy that Donald Trump exerted by traveling across the country, addressing massive sell-out "free" rallies. Look at the states. In the eleventh hour while Hillary was mostly MIA in key states, Trump was there at the right time. Remember when you look at this list, among other things, it is "Why Trump Got Elected!"

Primary rallies (June 2015–June 2016)

Date of Rally	City	State	Venue	Est.Vistors
Wed., June 17, 2015	Manchester	NH	Manchester Community College	300
Sat., July 11, 2015	Phoenix	AZ	Phoenix Convention Center	15,000
Tues., July 21, 2015	Sun City	SC	Magnolia Hall	500

Sat., July 25, 2015	Oskaloosa	IA	Oskaloosa High School	1,000
Fri., August 14, 2015	Hampton	NH	Winnacunnet High School	3,000
Fri., August 21, 2015	Mobile	AL	Ladd–Peebles Stadium	15,000-30,000
Tues., August 25, 2015	Dubuque	IA	Grand River Center	3,000
Thur., August 27, 2015	Greenville	SC	TD Convention Center	1,400
Fri., August 28, 2015	Norwood	MA	Home of Ernie Boch, Jr.	"1,500-2,000"
Mon., Sept. 14, 2015	Dallas	TX	American Airlines Center	15,000
Tues., Sept. 15, 2015	Los Angeles	CA	USS Iowa‼	1,000+
Fri., Sept. 25, 2015	Oklahoma City	OK	Oklahoma State Fair	15,000
Wed. Sept. 30, 2015	Keene	NH	Keene High School	3,500
Sat., Oct. 3, 2015	Franklin	TN	The Factory at Franklin	Thousands
Wed., Oct. 7, 2015	Waterloo	IA	Electric Park Ballroom	1,100
Sat., Oct. 10, 2015	Norcross	GA	North Atlanta Trade Center	7,700
Fri., Oct. 16, 2015	Tyngsboro	MA	Tyngsboro Elementary School	1,000+
Mon., Oct. 19, 2015	Anderson	SC	Civic Center of Anderson	5,000
Sat., Oct. 24, 2015	Jacksonville	FL	Jacksonville Landing	20,000
Tues., Oct. 27, 2015	Sioux City	IA	West High School	2,200
Thur., Oct. 29, 2015	Sparks	NV	Nugget Casino Resort	2,000
Sat., Oct. 31, 2015	Norfolk	VA	USS Wisconsin	2,000
Mon., Nov. 9, 2015	Springfield	IL	Prairie Capital Convention Center	10,200
Thur., Nov. 12, 2015	Fort Dodge	IA	Iowa Central Community College	1,500
Sat., Nov. 14, 2015	Beaumont	TX	Ford Arena	
Mon., Nov. 16, 2015	Knoxville	TN	Knoxville Convention Center	5,000
Wed., Nov. 18, 2015	Worcester	MA	DCU Center	10,500
Thur., Nov. 19, 2015	Newton	IA	Maytag Aud.DMACC Newton Campus	400
Sat., Nov. 21, 2015	Birmingham	AL	Birmingham–Jefferson Convention Complex	3,000
Mon., Nov. 23, 2015	Columbus	OH	Greater Columbus Convention Center	14,000
Tues., Nov. 24, 2015	Myrtle Beach	SC	Myrtle Beach Convention Center	8,000
Sat., Nov. 28, 2015	Sarasota	FL	Robarts Arena	9,000
Mon., Nov. 30, 2015	Macon	GA	Macon Coliseum	6,000

Tues., December 1, 2015	Waterville Val.	NH	White Mountain Athletic Club	900
Wed., December 2, 2015	Manassas	VA	Prince William County Fairgrounds	
Fri., December 4, 2015	Raleigh	NC	Dorton Arena	8,000
Sat., December 5, 2015	Davenport	IA	Mississippi Valley Fairgrounds	1,700
Sat., December 5, 2015	Spencer	IA	Clay County Regional Events Center	1,300
Mon., December 7, 2015	Mount Pleasant	SC	USS Yorktown	
Fri., December 11, 2015	Des Moines	IA	Varied Ind. Bldg, IA State Fairgrounds	2,500
Sat., December 12, 2015	Aiken	SC	USC Aiken Convocation Center	
Mon., December 14, 2015	Las Vegas	NV	Westgate Las Vegas Resort & Casino	
Wed., December 16, 2015	Mesa	AZ	Phoenix–Mesa Gateway Airport	3,100
Sat., December 19, 2015	Cedar Rapids	IA	Veterans Memorial Coliseum	1,200
Mon., December 21, 2015	Grand Rapids	MI	DeltaPlex Arena	7,000
Mon., December 28, 2015	Nashua	NH	Pennichuck Middle School	1,000
Tues., December 29, 2015	Council Bluffs	IA	Mid-America Center	
Wed., December 30, 2015	Hilton Head	SC	The Westin Hilton Head Island Resort & Spa	2,500
Sat., January 2, 2016	Biloxi	MS	Mississippi Coast Coliseum	15,000
Mon., January 4, 2016	Lowell	MA	Tsongas Center	Thousands
Tues., January 5, 2016	Claremont	NH	Stevens High School	1,200
Thur., January 7, 2016	Burlington	VT	Flynn Center for the Performing Arts	1,400
Fri., January 8, 2016	Rock Hill	SC	Winthrop Coliseum	6,500
Sat., January 9, 2016	Clear Lake	IA	Surf Ballroom	1,700
Sat., January 9, 2016	Ottumwa	IA	Bridgeview Center	
Sun., January 10, 2016	Reno	NV	Reno Events Center	4,000
Mon., January 11, 2016	Windham	NH	Castleton Banquet and Conference Center	550
Tues., January 12, 2016	Cedar Falls	IA	West Gym, Univ. of N. Iowa	2,000
Wed., January 13, 2016	Pensacola	FL	Pensacola Bay Center	10,000
Fri., January 15, 2016	Urbandale	IA	Living History Farms Visitor Center	100
Mon., January 18, 2016	Concord	NH	Concord High School	700
Mon., January 18, 2016	Lynchburg	VA	Vines Center, Liberty University	10,000

Tues., January 19, 2016	Ames	IA	Hansen Ag. Stu. Learning Center, IA ST UNIV	2,000
Wed., January 20, 2016	Norwalk	IA	The Wright Place	300
Wed., January 20, 2016	Tulsa	OK	Mabee Center, Oral Roberts University	9,000
Thur., January 21, 2016	Las Vegas	NV	South Point Hotel, Casino & Spa	3,000
Sat., January 23, 2016	Pella	IA	Douwstra Aud., Central College	400
Sat., January 23, 2016	Sioux Center	IA	B. J. Haan Aud. Dordt College	2,600
Sun., January 24, 2016	Muscatine	IA	Muscatine High School	1,000
Mon., January 25, 2016	Farmington	NH	Farmington Senior High School	1,000
Tues., January 26, 2016	Iowa City	IA	Iowa Field House, University of IA	2,000
Tues., January 26, 2016	Marshalltown	IA	RoundhouseGym, Marsh-alltown High School	2,149
Wed., January 27, 2016	Gilbert	SC	The Barn at Harmon's	400
Thur., January 28, 2016	Des Moines	IA	Sheslow Aud., Drake University	700
Fri., January 29, 2016	Nashua	NH	Radisson Hotel Nashua	850
Sat., January 30, 2016	Clinton	IA	Clinton Middle School	1,000
Sat., January 30, 2016	Davenport	IA	Adler Theatre	2,400
Sat., January 30, 2016	Dubuque	IA	Dubuque Regional Airport	1,200
Sun., January 31, 2016	Council Bluffs	IA	Gerald W. Kirn Middle School	2,000
Mon., February 1, 2016	Cedar Rapids	IA	DoubleTree Hotel Cedar Rapids Conv. Complex	1,500
Mon., February 1, 2016	Waterloo	IA	Ramada Waterloo Hotel and Convention Center	300
Tues., February 2, 2016	Milford	NH	Hampshire Hills Athletic Club	
Wed., February 3, 2016	Little Rock	AR	Barton Coliseum	11,500
Thur., February 4, 2016	Exeter	NH	Exeter Town Hall	
Thur., February 4, 2016	Portsmouth	NH	Great Bay Community College	500
Fri., February 5, 2016	Florence	SC	Florence Civic Center	Thousands
Sun., February 7, 2016	Holderness	NH	ALLWell N., Plymouth State University	2,500
Mon., February 8, 2016	Londonderry	NH	Londonderry Lions Club	200
Mon., February 8, 2016	Manchester	NH	Verizon Wireless Arena	5,000
Mon., February 8, 2016	Salem	NH	Derry-Salem Elks Lodge	200
Wed., February 10, 2016	Pendleton	SC	T. Ed Garrison Arena, Clemson Univ.	5,000

Thur., February 11, 2016	Baton Rouge	LA	Baton Rouge River Center	10,000
Fri., February 12, 2016	Tampa	FL	USFSunDome, University of South Florida	10,000
Mon., February 15, 2016	Greenville	SC	TD Convention Center	Thousands
Tues., February 16, 2016	Beaufort	SC	Beaufort HS Performing Arts Center	20,000
Tues., February 16, 2016	North Augusta	SC	Riverview Park Activities Center	2,000
Wed., February 17, 2016	Sumter	SC	Sumter County Civic Center	4,000
Wed., February 17, 2016	Walterboro	SC	Randy and Sara White's farm	4,000
Thur., February 18, 2016	Gaffney	SC	Broad River Electric Cooperative	
Thur., February 18, 2016	Kiawah	SC	TurtlePointClubhouse, Kiawah Isl. Golf Resort	
Fri., February 19, 2016	N. Charleston	SC	North Charleston Convention Center	2,000
Fri., February 19, 2016	Myrtle Beach	SC	Myrtle Beach Sports Center	12,000
Fri., February 19, 2016	Pawleys Island	SC	Pawley's Plantation Golf & Country Club	1,000
Sun., February 21, 2016	Atlanta	GA	Georgia World Congress Center	
Mon., February 22, 2016	Las Vegas	NV	South Point Hotel, Casino & Spa	
Tues., February 23, 2016	Sparks	NV	Rose Ballroom	3,016
Fri., February 26, 2016	Oklahoma City	OK	Cox Convention Center	7,000
Sat., February 27, 2016	Highfill	AR	Northwest Arkansas Regional Airport	5,000
Sat., February 27, 2016	Fort Worth	TX	Fort Worth Convention Center	8,000
Sat., February 27, 2016	Millington	TN	Millington Regional Jetport	10,000
Sun., February 28, 2016	Madison	AL	Madison City Schools Stadium	
Mon., February 29, 2016	Radford	VA	Dedmon Center, Radford University	3,800
Mon., February 29, 2016	Valdosta	GA	The Complex, Valdosta State University	7,500
Tues., March 1, 2016	Columbus	OH	Port Columbus International Airport	4,000
Tues., March 1, 2016	Louisville	KY	Kentucky International Convention Center	5,000
Thur., March 3, 2016	Portland	ME	The Westin Portland Harborview Hotel	1,100
Fri., March 4, 2016	Warren	MI	Sports&ExpoCtr, Macomb Comm. College	4,000
Fri., March 4, 2016	Cadillac	MI	Wexford County Civic Center	3,500

Fri., March 4, 2016	New Orleans	LA	Lakefront Airport	4,000
Sat., March 5, 2016	Orlando	FL	CFE Arena, University of Central Florida	10,000
Sat., March 5, 2016	Wichita	KS	CenturyII Performing Arts & Convention Center	
Mon., March 7, 2016	Concord	NC	Cabarrus Arena & Events Center	3,000
Mon., March 7, 2016	Madison	MS	Madison Central High School	9,000
Wed., March 9, 2016	Fayetteville	NC	Crown Coliseum	11,000
Fri., March 11, 2016	St. Louis	MO	Peabody Opera House	3,100
Sat., March 12, 2016	Cleveland	OH	I-X Center	29,000
Sat., March 12, 2016	Dayton	OH	Dayton International Airport	20,000
Sat., March 12, 2016	Kansas City	MO	Midland Theatre	7,000
Sun., March 13, 2016	Bloomington	IL	Synergy Flight Ctr, Cent. Illinois Reg. Airport	3,000
Sun., March 13, 2016	Boca Raton	FL	Sunset Cove Amph., Sugar Sand Park	6,000
Mon., March 14, 2016	Tampa	FL	Tampa Convention Center	1,500
Mon., March 14, 2016	Vienna	OH	Winner, Youngstown–Warren Airport	2,500
Fri., March 18, 2016	Salt Lake City	UT	Inifinity Event Center	1,200
Sat., March 19, 2016	Fountain Hills	AZ	Fountain Park	10,000
Sat., March 19, 2016	Tucson	AZ	Tucson Convention Center	5,000
Tues., March 29, 2016	Janesville	WI	Janesville Conference Center	1,000
Wed., March 30, 2016	Appleton	WI	Radisson Paper Valley Hotel	1,000
Wed., March 30, 2016	De Pere	WI	Byron L. Walter Theatre, St. Norbert Coll.	750
Sat., April 2, 2016	Eau Claire	WI	Memorial High School	1,500
Sat., April 2, 2016	Racine	WI	Memorial Hall	1,200
Sat., April 2, 2016	Rothschild	WI	Central Wiscon. Conv. & Expo Center	1,700
Sun., April 3, 2016	West Allis	WI	Nathan Hale High School	1,000
Mon., April 4, 2016	La Crosse	WI	La Crosse Center	1,700
Mon., April 4, 2016	Milwaukee	WI	Milwaukee Theatre	
Mon., April 4, 2016	Superior	WI	Richard I. Bong Airport	1,000
Wed., April 6, 2016	Bethpage	NY	Grumman Studios	10,000
Sun., April 10, 2016	Rochester	NY	JetSmart, Rochester Int. Airport	9,000
Mon., April 11, 2016	Albany	NY	Times Union Center	10,000

Tues., April 12, 2016	Rome	NY	Griffiss International Airport	5,000
Wed., April 13, 2016	Pittsburgh	PA	David L. Lawrence Convention Center	4,500
Fri., April 15, 2016	Hartford	CT	Connecticut Convention Center	7,000
Fri., April 15, 2016	Plattsburgh	NY	Crete Civic Center	3,000
Sat., April 16, 2016	Syracuse	NY	Nick J. Pirro Convention Center, Oncenter	5,000
Sat., April 16, 2016	Watertown	NY	Watertown International Airport	2,000
Sun., April 17, 2016	Poughkeepsie	NY	Mid-Hudson Civic Center	
Mon., April 18, 2016	Buffalo	NY	First Niagara Center	11,400
Wed., April 20, 2016	Indianapolis	IN	Financial Pav., Indiana St. Fairgrounds	4,000
Wed., April 20, 2016	Berlin	MD	Stephen Decatur High School	3,000
Thur., April 21, 2016	Harrisburg	PA	Pennsylvania Farm Show Complex & Expo Center	6,000
Fri., April 22, 2016	Harrington	DE	Quillen Arena, Delaware State Fairgrounds	8,200
Sat., April 23, 2016	Bridgeport	CT	Klein Memorial Auditorium	1,400
Sat., April 23, 2016	Waterbury	CT	Crosby High School	3,000
Sun., April 24, 2016	Hagerstown	MD	Rider Jet Ctr, Hagerstown Reg. Airport	5,000
Mon., April 25, 2016	Warwick	RI	Crowne Plaza Hotel Providence-Warwick	1,000
Mon., April 25, 2016	West Chester	PA	West Chester University	3,500
Mon., April 25, 2016	Wilkes-Barre	PA	Mohegan Sun Arena at Casey Plaza	10,000
Wed., April 27, 2016	Indianapolis	IN	Indiana Farmers Coliseum	5,000
Thur., April 28, 2016	Costa Mesa	CA	Pacific Amphitheatre, OC Fair & Event Center	
Thur., April 28, 2016	Evansville	IN	Old National Events Plaza	12,000
Sun., May 1, 2016	Fort Wayne	IN	Allen County War Memorial Coliseum	8,000
Sun., May 1, 2016	Terre Haute	IN	Indiana Theatre	2,100
Mon., May 2, 2016	Carmel	IN	Palladium at the Center for the Performing Arts	1,800
Mon., May 2, 2016	South Bend	IN	Century Center	8,000
Thur., May 5, 2016	Charleston	WV	Charleston Civic Center	
Fri., May 6, 2016	Eugene	OR	Lane Events Center	5,000
Fri., May 6, 2016	Omaha	NE	Werner Ent., Eppley Airfield	3,500

Sat., May 7, 2016	Lynden	WA	Northwest Washington Fair and Event Center	7,500
Sat., May 7, 2016	Spokane	WA	Spokane Convention Center	10,000
Tues., May 24, 2016	Albuquerque	NM	Albuquerque Convention Center	8,000
Wed., May 25, 2016	Anaheim	CA	Anaheim Convention Center	3,000
Thur., May 26, 2016	Billings	MT	Rimrock Auto Arena at MetraPark	7,000
Fri., May 27, 2016	Fresno	CA	Selland Arena	7,000
Fri., May 27, 2016	San Diego	CA	San Diego Convention Center	
Wed., June 1, 2016	Sacramento	CA	Jet Center, Sacramento International Airport	5,000
Thur., June 2, 2016	San Jose	CA	South Hall, San Jose Convention Center	
Fri., June 3, 2016	Redding	CA	Redding Municipal Airport	4,000

General election rallies (June 2016–Nov. 2016)

Date of Rally	City	State	Venue	Estimated Visitors
Fri., June 10, 2016	Richmond	VA	Richmond Coliseum	5,000
Sat., June 11, 2016	Moon	PA	Pittsburgh International Airport	1,500
Sat., June 11, 2016	Tampa	FL	Tampa Convention Center	4,000
Tues., June 14, 2016	Greensboro	NC	Greensboro Coliseum Complex	6,150
Wed., June 15, 2016	Atlanta	GA	Fox Theatre	3,500
Thur., June 16, 2016	Dallas	TX	Gilley's Club	3,600
Fri., June 17, 2016	The Woodlands	TX	Woodlands Waterway Marriott	5,000
Sat., June 18, 2016	Las Vegas	NV	Mystère, Treasure Island Hotel	1,600
Sat., June 18, 2016	Phoenix	AZ	Ariz. Veterans Mem. Coliseum, Az. St Fair	6,000
Tues., June 28, 2016	St. Clairsville	OH	Health and Phys Ed Ctr, Ohio Univ.	4,000
Wed., June 29, 2016	Bangor	ME	Cross Insurance Center	4,000
Tues., July 5, 2016	Raleigh	NC	Raleigh Mem. Aud, Duke Energy Center	2,250
Wed., July 6, 2016	Cincinnati	OH	Sharonville Convention Center	7,000
Tues., July 12, 2016	Westfield	IN	Grand Park Event Center, Grand Park	2,000
Mon., July 25, 2016	Winston-Salem	NC	Winston-Salem / Dixie Classic Fairgrounds	4,728

Wed., July 27, 2016	Scranton	PA	Student Union Gym, Lackawanna Coll.	3,500
Wed., July 27, 2016	Toledo	OH	Huntington Center	8,879
Thur., July 28, 2016	Cedar Rapids	IA	DoubleTree Hotel Cedar Rapids Conv. Complex	3,000
Thur., July 28, 2016	Davenport	IA	Adler Theatre	2,400
Fri., July 29, 2016	Colorado Springs	CO	Gallogly Event Ctr, Univ of Col. Colorado Springs	2,500
Fri., July 29, 2016	Denver	CO	Wings Over the Rockies Air and Space Museum	6,000
Mon., August 1, 2016	Columbus	OH	Greater Columbus Convention Center	1,000
Mon., August 1, 2016	Mechanicsburg	PA	Cumberland Valley High School	5,000
Tues., August 2, 2016	Ashburn	VA	Briar Woods High School	800
Wed., August 3, 2016	Daytona Beach	FL	Ocean Center	10,000
Wed., August 3, 2016	Jacksonville	FL	Jacksonville Veterans Memorial Arena	10,000
Thur., August 4, 2016	Portland	ME	Merrill Auditorium	1,600
Fri., August 5, 2016	Des Moines	IA	Iowa Events Center	6,000
Fri., August 5, 2016	Green Bay	WI	KI Convention Center	3,000
Sat., August 6, 2016	Windham	NH	Windham High School	1,500
Tues., August 9, 2016	Fayetteville	NC	Crown Arena	3,000
Tues., August 9, 2016	Wilmington	NC	Trask Coliseum. Univ. NC Wilmington	
Wed., August 10, 2016	Sunrise	FL	BB&T Center	
Thur., August 11, 2016	Kissimmee	FL	Silver Spurs Arena	8,000
Fri., August 12, 2016	Altoona	PA	Blair County Convention Center	5,000
Fri., August 12, 2016	Erie	PA	Erie Insurance Arena	8,000
Sat., August 13, 2016	Fairfield	CT	William H. Pitt Ctr, Sacred Heart Univ.	5,000
Tues., August 16, 2016	West Bend	WI	Ziegler Family, Wash Cty Fair Park /Conf Ctr	2,000
Thur., August 18, 2016	Charlotte	NC	Charlotte Convention Center	5,000
Fri., August 19, 2016	Dimondale	MI	The Summit Sports and Ice Complex	5,000
Sat., August 20, 2016	Fredericksburg	VA	Fredericksburg Expo & Conference Center	3,600
Mon., August 22, 2016	Akron	OH	James A. Rhodes Arena, Univ. of Akron	5,000
Tues., August 23, 2016	Austin	TX	Luedecke Arena	7,000
Wed., August 24, 2016	Tampa	FL	Entertainment Hall, FS Fairgrounds	3,000
Wed., August 24, 2016	Jackson	MS	Mississippi Coliseum	

Thur., August 25, 2016	Manchester	NH	Radisson Hotel Manchester Downtown	850
Tues., August 30, 2016	Everett	WA	Xfinity Arena	
Wed., August 31, 2016	Phoenix	AZ	Phoenix Convention Center	7,502
Thur., Sept. 1, 2016	Wilmington	OH	Roberts Centre	5,500
Tues., Sept. 6, 2016	Greenville	NC	Greenville Convention Center	3,000
Fri., Sept. 9, 2016	Pensacola	FL	Pensacola Bay Center	12,500
Mon., Sept. 12, 2016	Asheville	NC	U.S. Cellular Center	6,000
Tues., Sept. 13, 2016	Clive	IA	7 Flags Event Center	1,600
Wed., Sept. 14, 2016	Canton	OH	Canton Memorial Civic Center	6,000
Thur., Sept. 15, 2016	Laconia	NH	Laconia Middle School	600
Fri., Sept. 16, 2016	Miami	FL	Knight Center Complex	
Sat., Sept. 17, 2016	Colorado Springs	CO	Colorado Jet Center, Colorado Springs Airport	
Mon., Sept. 19, 2016	Estero	FL	Germain Arena	8,000
Tues., Sept. 20, 2016	High Point	NC	Millis Ath. Conv. Center, High Point Univ.	2,000
Tues., Sept. 20, 2016	Kenansville	NC	Duplin County Events Center	6,000
Wed., Sept. 21, 2016	Toledo	OH	Stranahan Theater	
Thur., Sept. 22, 2016	Chester Twp	PA	Sun Center Studios	3000+
Sat., Sept. 24, 2016	Roanoke	VA	Berglund Center	9,000
Tues., Sept. 27, 2016	Melbourne	FL	Orlando Melbourne International Airport	
Wed., Sept. 28, 2016	Council Bluffs	IA	Mid-America Center	1,200
Wed., Sept. 28, 2016	Waukesha	WI	Waukesha County Expo Center	1,500
Thur., Sept. 29, 2016	Bedford	NH	NH Sportsplex	850
Fri., Sept. 30, 2016	Novi	MI	Suburban Collection Showplace	6,000
Sat., Oct. 1, 2016	Manheim	PA	Spooky Nook Sports	6,000
Mon., Oct. 3, 2016	Pueblo	CO	Pueblo Convention Center	2,000
Mon., Oct. 3, 2016	Loveland	CO	Budweiser Events Center	8,000
Tues., Oct. 4, 2016	Prescott Valley	AZ	Prescott Valley Event Center	7,000
Wed., Oct. 5, 2016	Henderson	NV	Henderson Pavilion	7,000
Wed., Oct. 5, 2016	Reno	NV	Reno-Sparks Convention Center	

Mon., Oct. 10, 2016	Ambridge	PA	Ambridge Area High School	3,000
Mon., Oct. 10, 2016	Wilkes-Barre	PA	Mohegan Sun Arena at Casey Plaza	9,000
Tues., Oct. 11, 2016	Panama City Beach	FL	Aaron Bessant Amphitheater, Aaron Bessant Park	8,500
Wed., Oct. 12, 2016	Ocala	FL	Southeastern Livestock Pavilion	12,000
Wed., Oct. 12, 2016	Lakeland	FL	Lakeland Linder Regional Airport	7,000
Thur., Oct. 13, 2016	West Palm Beach	FL	South Florida Fairgrounds Expo Center	6,000
Thur., Oct. 13, 2016	Cincinnati	OH	U.S. Bank Arena	
Fri., Oct. 14, 2016	Greensboro	NC	White Oak Amphitheatre	4,000
Fri., Oct. 14, 2016	Charlotte	NC	Charlotte Convention Center	5,000
Sat., Oct. 15, 2016	Portsmouth	NH	Toyota of Portsmouth	7,000
Sat., Oct. 15, 2016	Bangor	ME	Cross Insurance Center	4,000
Mon., Oct. 17, 2016	Green Bay	WI	KI Convention Center	3,000
Tues., Oct. 18, 2016	Colorado Springs	CO	Norris-Penrose Event Center	
Tues., Oct. 18, 2016	Grand Junction	CO	West Star Aviat., Grand Junction Reg Airport	
Thur., Oct. 20, 2016	Delaware	OH	Delaware County Fair	1,500
Fri., Oct. 21, 2016	Fletcher	NC	WNC Agricultural Center	3,100
Fri., Oct. 21, 2016	Johnstown	PA	Cambria County War Memorial Arena	4,000
Fri., Oct. 21, 2016	Newtown Township	PA	Newtown Athletic Club Sports Training Center	4,000
Sat., Oct. 22, 2016	Virginia Beach	VA	Library Plaza, Regent University	10,000
Sat., Oct. 22, 2016	Cleveland	OH	I-X Center	
Sun., Oct. 23, 2016	Naples	FL	Collier County Fairgrounds	12,000
Mon., Oct. 24, 2016	St. Augustine	FL	St. Augustine Amphitheatre	
Mon., Oct. 24, 2016	Tampa	FL	MidFlorida Credit Union Amphitheatre	>15,000-28,000
Tues., Oct. 25, 2016	Sanford	FL	Million Air, Or/Sanford Int. Airport	10,000
Tues., Oct. 25, 2016	Tallahassee	FL	Tallahassee Car Museum	
Wed., Oct. 26, 2016	Kinston	NC	Jet Center, Kinston Regional Jetport	3,100
Thur., Oct. 27, 2016	Springfield	OH	Clark County Fairgrounds	5,000
Thur., Oct. 27, 2016	Toledo	OH	SeaGate Convention Centre	2,850

Thur., Oct. 27, 2016	Geneva	OH	Track and Field Building, SPIRE Institute	5,000
Fri., Oct. 28, 2016	Manchester	NH	Radisson Hotel Manchester Downtown	
Fri., Oct. 28, 2016	Lisbon	ME	Open Door Christian Academy	1,200
Fri., Oct. 28, 2016	Cedar Rapids	IA	McGrath Amphitheatre	5,000
Sat., Oct. 29, 2016	Golden	CO	Jefferson County Events Center	[338][339]
Sat., Oct. 29, 2016	Phoenix	AZ	Phoenix Convention Center	8,000
Sun., Oct. 30, 2016	Las Vegas	NV	The Venetian Las Vegas	8,400
Sun., Oct. 30, 2016	Greeley	CO	Bank Arena, Univ. of N. Colorado	3000
Sun., Oct. 30, 2016	Albuquerque	NM	Atlantic Aviation ABQ Int.	4,000
Mon., Oct. 31, 2016	Grand Rapids	MI	DeltaPlex Arena	6,500
Mon., Oct. 31, 2016	Warren	MI	Sports Cent. Macomb Comm. Coll. S. Campus	5,000
Tues., Nov. 1, 2016	Eau Claire	WI	W.L. Zorn Arena	3,000
Wed., Nov. 2, 2016	Orlando	FL	CFE Arena, Central Florida Fairgrounds	10,000
Wed., Nov. 2, 2016	Pensacola	FL	Maritime Park Hunter Amph	10,000
Wed., Nov. 2, 2016	Miami	FL	Bayfront Park	2,600
Thur., Nov. 3, 2016	Jacksonville	FL	Jacksonville Equestrian Center	4,000
Thur., Nov. 3, 2016	Concord	NC	Cabarrus Arena & Events Center	4,200
Thur., Nov. 3, 2016	Selma	NC	The Farm	15,000
Fri., Nov. 4, 2016	Atkinson	NH	Atkinson Country Club	1,000
Fri., Nov. 4, 2016	Wilmington	OH	Airborne Maintenance & Eng. Services, Inc	3,000
Fri., Nov. 4, 2016	Hershey	PA	Giant Center	13,000
Sat., Nov. 5, 2016	Tampa	FL	Florida State Fairgrounds	20,000
Sat., Nov. 5, 2016	Wilmington	NC	Wilmington International Airport	5,000
Sat., Nov. 5, 2016	Reno	NV	Reno-Sparks Convention Center	8,000
Sat., Nov. 5, 2016	Denver	CO	National Western Complex	8,000
Sun., Nov. 6, 2016	Sioux City	IA	Sioux City Convention Center	4,300
Sun., Nov. 6, 2016	Minneapolis	MN	Sun Country Airlines	20,000
Sun., Nov. 6, 2016	Sterling Heights	MI	Freedom Hill Amph., County Park	8,000
Sun., Nov. 6, 2016	Moon Township	PA	Atlantic Aviation	12,000

Sun., Nov. 6, 2016	Leesburg	VA	Agricultural hall, Loudoun Fairgrounds	20,000
Mon., Nov. 7, 2016	Sarasota	FL	Robarts, Sarasota Cty Fairgrounds	5,000
Mon., Nov. 7, 2016	Raleigh	NC	Dorton Arena	7,000
Mon., Nov. 7, 2016	Scranton	PA	Lackawanna Coll. Stu. Union	5,000
Mon., Nov. 7, 2016	Manchester	NH	SNHU Arena	12,000
Mon., Nov. 7, 2016	Grand Rapids	MI	DeVos Place Convention Center	4,200

Think about all the hard work preparing for and speaking at all those great rallies. That's "Why Trump Got Elected!"

Chapter 8 Trump's Trip Down the Escalator

Donald Trump's Presidential Announcement

June 16, 2015

Think about a guy, mostly unscripted talking from the heart to the American people. Then, as you read his speech, along with all Trump supporters, you too will know Why Trump Got Elected!

Here we go right below:

Wow. Whoa. That is some group of people. Thousands.
So nice, thank you very much. That's really nice. Thank you. It's great to be at Trump Tower. It's great to be in a wonderful city, New York. And it's an honor to have everybody here. This is beyond anybody's expectations. There's been no crowd like this.

And, I can tell, some of the candidates, they went in. They didn't know the air-conditioner didn't work. They sweated like dogs.

They didn't know the room was too big, because they didn't have anybody there. How are they going to beat ISIS? I don't think it's gonna happen.

Our country is in serious trouble. We don't have victories anymore. We used to have victories, but we don't have them. When was the last time anybody saw us beating, let's say, China in a trade deal? They kill us. I beat China all the time. All the time.

When did we beat Japan at anything? They send their cars over by the millions, and what do we do? When was the last time you saw a Chevrolet in Tokyo? It doesn't exist, folks. They beat us all the time.

When do we beat Mexico at the border? They're laughing at us, at our stupidity. And now they are beating us economically. They are not our friend, believe me. But they're killing us economically.

The U.S. has become a dumping ground for everybody else's problems.

Thank you. It's true, and these are the best and the finest. When Mexico sends its people, they're not sending their best. They're not sending you. They're not sending you. They're sending people that have lots of problems, and they're bringing those problems with us. They're bringing drugs. They're bringing crime. They're rapists. And some, I assume, are good people.

[By reflecting the sentiments of many Americans, candidate Trump quickly gained support from normal Americans and he kept it through today with all the Russia crap. That's Why Trump Got Elected.]

But I speak to border guards and they tell us what we're getting. And it only makes common sense. It only makes common sense. They're sending us not the right people.

It's coming from more than Mexico. It's coming from all over South and Latin America, and it's coming probably— probably— from the Middle East. But we don't know. Because we have no protection and we have no competence, we don't know what's happening. And it's got to stop, and it's got to stop fast.

Islamic terrorism is eating up large portions of the Middle East. They've become rich. I'm in competition with them.

They just built a hotel in Syria. Can you believe this? They built a hotel. When I have to build a hotel, I pay interest. They don't have to pay interest, because they took the oil that, when we left Iraq, I said we should've taken.

So now ISIS has the oil, and what they don't have, Iran has. And in 19— and I will tell you this, and I said it very strongly, years ago, I said— and I love the military, and I want to have the strongest military that we've ever had, and we need it more now than ever. But I said, "Don't hit Iraq," because you're going to totally destabilize the Middle East. Iran is going to take over the Middle East, Iran and somebody else will get the oil, and it turned out that Iran is now taking over Iraq. Think of it. Iran is taking over Iraq, and they're taking it over big league.

We spent $2 trillion in Iraq, $2 trillion. We lost thousands of lives, thousands in Iraq. We have wounded soldiers, who I love, I love — they're great — all over the place, thousands and thousands of wounded soldiers.

And we have nothing. We can't even go there. We have nothing. And every time we give Iraq equipment, the first time a bullet goes off in the air, they leave it.

Last week, I read 2,300 Humvees— these are big vehicles— were left behind for the enemy. 2,000? You would say maybe two, maybe four? 2,300 sophisticated vehicles, they ran, and the enemy took them.

Last quarter, it was just announced our gross domestic product— a sign of strength, right? But not for us. It was below zero. Whoever heard of this? It's never below zero.

Our labor participation rate was the worst since 1978. But think of it, GDP below zero, horrible labor participation rate.

[In this first of hundreds of campaign speeches, Mr. Trump set the theme for his presidency. He focused on the sins of the last administration He portrayed Obama and Company as being inept on the foreign policy as well as the domestic policy. He is very convincing. Before he had even once said, "Let's make America great again," he noted how bad things had become with a guy who cared little about America at the helm. The people were convinced. Americans want America to be great—not also-rans. That's "Why Trump Got Elected!"]

And our real unemployment is anywhere from 18 to 20 percent. Don't believe the 5.6. Don't believe it.

That's right. A lot of people up there can't get jobs. They can't get jobs, because there are no jobs, because China has our jobs and Mexico has our jobs. They all have jobs.

But the real number, the real number is anywhere from 18 to 19 and maybe even 21 percent, and nobody talks about it, because it's a statistic that's full of nonsense.

Our enemies are getting stronger and stronger by the way, and we as a country are getting weaker. Even our nuclear arsenal doesn't work.

It came out recently they have equipment that is 30 years old. They don't know if it worked. And I thought it was horrible when it was broadcast on television, because boy, does that send signals to Putin and all of the other people that look at us and they say, "That is a group of people, and that is a nation that truly has no clue. They don't know what they're doing. They don't know what they're doing."

We have a disaster called the big lie: Obamacare. Obamacare.

Yesterday, it came out that costs are going for people up 29, 39, 49, and even 55 percent, and deductibles are through the roof. You have to be hit by a tractor, literally, a tractor, to use it, because the deductibles are so high, it's virtually useless. It's virtually useless. It is a disaster.

And remember the $5 billion website? $5 billion we spent on a website, and to this day it doesn't work. A $5 billion website.

I have so many websites, I have them all over the place. I hire people, they do a website. It costs me [nowhere close to $5 billion for just one website.]

Well, you need somebody, because politicians are all talk, no action. Nothing's gonna get done. They will not bring us— believe me— to the promised land. They will not.

As an example, I've been on the circuit making speeches, and I hear my fellow Republicans. And they're wonderful people. I like them. They all want me to support them. They don't know how to bring it about. They come up to my office. I'm meeting with three of them in the next week. And they don't know— "Are you running? Are you not running? Could we have your support? What do we do? How do we do it?"

I like them. And I hear their speeches. And they don't talk jobs and they don't talk China. When was the last time you heard China is killing us? They're devaluing their currency to a level that you wouldn't believe. It makes it impossible for our companies to compete, impossible. They're killing us.

But you don't hear that from anybody else. You don't hear it from anybody else. And I watch the speeches.

I watch the speeches of these people, and they say the sun will rise, the moon will set, all sorts of wonderful things will happen. And people are saying, "What's going on? I just want a job. Just get me a job. I don't need the rhetoric. I want a job."

And that's what's happening. And it's going to get worse, because remember, Obamacare really kicks in in '16, 2016. Obama is going to be out playing golf. He might be on one of my courses. I would invite him, I actually would say. I have the best courses in the world, so I'd say, you what, if he wants to— I have one right next to the White House, right on the Potomac. If he'd like to play, that's fine.

In fact, I'd love him to leave early and play, that would be a very good thing.

But Obamacare kicks in in 2016. Really big league. It is going to be amazingly destructive. Doctors are quitting. I have a friend who's a doctor, and he said to me the other day, "Donald, I never saw anything like it. I have more accountants than I have nurses. It's a disaster. My patients are beside themselves. They had a plan that was good. They have no plan now."

We have to repeal Obamacare, and it can be— and— and it can be replaced with something much better for everybody. Let it be for everybody. But much better and much less expensive for people and for the government. And we can do it.

[Trump knows the crooked polls that praise Obamacare are bogus. That's "Why Trump Got Elected!"]

So, I've watched the politicians. I've dealt with them all my life. If you can't make a good deal with a politician, then there's something wrong with you. You're certainly not very good. And that's what we have representing us. They will never make America great again. They don't even have a chance. They're controlled fully— they're controlled fully by the lobbyists, by the donors, and by the special interests, fully.

[The people know that their representatives are representing themselves and That's Why Trump Got Elected.]

Yes, they control them. Hey, I have lobbyists. I have to tell you. I have lobbyists that can produce anything for me. They're great. But you know what? It won't happen. It won't happen. Because we have to stop doing things for some people, but for this country, it's destroying our country. We have to stop, and it has to stop now.

Now, our country needs— our country needs a truly great leader, and we need a truly great leader now. We need a leader that wrote "The Art of the Deal."
We need a leader that can bring back our jobs, can bring back our manufacturing, can bring back our military, can take care of our vets. Our vets have been abandoned.

[Donald Trump connected with the people by speaking the peoples' language and by focusing on things that Americans know are not right. That's "Why Donald Trump Got Elected!"]

And we also need a cheerleader.

You know, when President Obama was elected, I said, "Well, the one thing, I think he'll do well. I think he'll be a great cheerleader for the country. I think he'd be a great spirit."

He was vibrant. He was young. I really thought that he would be a great cheerleader.
He's not a leader. That's true. You're right about that.

But he wasn't a cheerleader either. He's actually a negative force. He's been a negative force. He wasn't a cheerleader; he was the opposite.

We need somebody that can take the brand of the United States and make it great again. It's not great again.

We need— we need somebody— we need somebody that literally will take this country and make it great again. We can do that.

And, I will tell you, I love my life. I have a wonderful family. They're saying, "Dad, you're going to do something that's going to be so tough."

You know, all of my life, I've heard that a truly successful person, a really, really successful person and even modestly successful cannot run for public office. Just can't happen. And yet that's the kind of mindset that you need to make this country great again.

So, ladies and gentlemen…I am officially running… for president of the United States, and we are going to make our country great again.

It can happen. Our country has tremendous potential. We have tremendous people.

We have people that aren't working. We have people that have no incentive to work. But they're going to have incentive to work, because the greatest social program is a job. And they'll be proud, and they'll love it, and they'll make much more than they would've ever made, and they'll be— they'll be doing so well, and we're going to be thriving as a country, thriving. It can happen.

I will be the greatest jobs president that God ever created. I tell you that.

I'll bring back our jobs from China, from Mexico, from Japan, from so many places. I'll bring back our jobs, and I'll bring back our money.

Right now, think of this: We owe China $1.3 trillion. We owe Japan more than that. So, they come in, they take our jobs, they take our money, and then they loan us back the money, and we pay them in interest, and then the dollar goes up so their deal's even better.

How stupid are our leaders? How stupid are these politicians to allow this to happen? How stupid are they?

I'm going to tell you— thank you. I'm going to tell you a couple of stories about trade, because I'm totally against the trade bill for a number of reasons.

Number one, the people negotiating don't have a clue. Our president doesn't have a clue. He's a bad negotiator.

He's the one that did Bergdahl. We get Bergdahl, they get five killer terrorists that everybody wanted over there.

We get Bergdahl. We get a traitor. We get a no-good traitor, and they get the five people that they wanted for years, and those people are now back on the battlefield trying to kill us. That's the negotiator we have.

Take a look at the deal he's making with Iran. He makes that deal, Israel maybe won't exist very long. It's a disaster, and we have to protect Israel. But...

So, we need people— I'm a free trader. But the problem with free trade is you need really talented people to negotiate for you. If you don't have talented people, if you don't have great leadership, if you don't have people that know business, not just a political hack that got the job because he made a contribution to a campaign, which is the way all jobs, just about, are gotten, free trade terrible.

Free trade can be wonderful if you have smart people, but we have people that are stupid. We have people that aren't smart. And we have people that are controlled by special interests. And it's just not going to work.

So, here's a couple of stories happened recently. A friend of mine is a great manufacturer. And, you know, China comes over and they dump all their stuff, and I buy it. I buy it, because, frankly, I have an obligation to buy it, because they devalue their currency so brilliantly, they just did it recently, and nobody thought they could do it again.

But with all our problems with Russia, with all our problems with everything— everything, they got away with it again. And it's impossible for our people here to compete.

So, I want to tell you this story. A friend of mine who's a great manufacturer, calls me up a few weeks ago. He's very upset. I said, "What's your problem?"

He said, "You know, I make great product."
And I said, "I know. I know that because I buy the product."

He said, "I can't get it into China. They won't accept it. I sent a boat over and they actually sent it back. They talked about environmental, they talked about all sorts of crap that had nothing to do with it."

I said, "Oh, wait a minute, that's terrible. Does anyone know this?"

He said, "Yeah, they do it all the time with other people."

I said, "They send it back?"

"Yeah. So, I finally got it over there and they charged me a big tariff. They're not supposed to be doing that. I told them."

Now, they do charge you tariff on trucks, when we send trucks and other things over there.

Ask Boeing. They wanted Boeing's secrets. They wanted their patents and all their secrets before they agreed to buy planes from Boeing.

Hey, I'm not saying they're stupid. I like China. I sell apartments for— I just sold an apartment for $15 million to somebody from China. Am I supposed to dislike them? I own a big chunk of the Bank of America

Building at 1290 Avenue of the Americas, that I got from China in a war. Very valuable.

I love China. The biggest bank in the world is from China. You know where their United States headquarters is located? In this building, in Trump Tower. I love China. People say, "Oh, you don't like China?"

No, I love them. But their leaders are much smarter than our leaders, and we can't sustain ourselves with that. There's too much— it's like— it's like take the New England Patriots and Tom Brady and have them play your high school football team. That's the difference between China's leaders and our leaders.

They are ripping us. We are rebuilding China. We're rebuilding many countries. China, you go there now, roads, bridges, schools, you never saw anything like it. They have bridges that make the George Washington Bridge look like small potatoes. And they're all over the place.

We have all the cards, but we don't know how to use them. We don't even know that we have the cards, because our leaders don't understand the game. We could turn off that spigot by charging them tax until they behave properly.

[Trump talked to the people like it was a fireside chat or a chat with a neighbor. He makes his points. Normal people got the message. It was easy to get. "That's Why Trump Got Elected!"]

Now they're going militarily. They're building a military island in the middle of the South China sea. A military island. Now, our country could never do that because we'd have to get environmental clearance, and the environmentalist wouldn't let our country— we would never build in an ocean. They built it in about one year, this massive military port.

They're building up their military to a point that is very scary. You have a problem with ISIS. You have a bigger problem with China.

And, in my opinion, the new China, believe it or not, in terms of trade, is Mexico.

So, this man tells me about the manufacturing. I say, "That's a terrible story. I hate to hear it."

But I have another one, Ford.

So, Mexico takes a company, a car company that was going to build in Tennessee, rips it out. Everybody thought the deal was dead. Reported it in the Wall Street Journal recently. Everybody thought it was a done deal. It's going in and that's going to be it, going into Tennessee. Great state, great people.

All of a sudden, at the last moment, this big car manufacturer, foreign, announces they're not going to Tennessee. They're gonna spend their $1 billion in Mexico instead. Not good.

Now, Ford announces a few weeks ago that Ford is going to build a $2.5 billion car and truck and parts manufacturing plant in Mexico. $2.5 billion, it's going to be one of the largest in the world. Ford. Good company.

So I announced that I'm running for president. I would…

… one of the early things I would do, probably before I even got in— and I wouldn't even use— you know, I have— I know the smartest negotiators in the world. I know the good ones. I know the bad ones. I know the overrated ones.

You get a lot of them that are overrated. They're not good. They think they are. They get good stories, because the newspapers get buffaloed. But they're not good.

But I know the negotiators in the world, and I put them one for each country. Believe me, folks. We will do very, very well, very, very well.

But I wouldn't even waste my time with this one. I would call up the head of Ford, who I know. If I was president, I'd say, "Congratulations. I understand that you're building a nice $2.5 billion car factory in Mexico and that you're going to take your cars and sell them to the United States zero tax, just flow them across the border."

And you say to yourself, "How does that help us," right? "How does that help us? Where is that good"? It's not.

So, I would say, "Congratulations. That's the good news. Let me give you the bad news. Every car and every truck and every part manufactured in this plant that comes across the border, we're going to charge you a 35-percent tax, and that tax is going to be paid simultaneously with the transaction, and that's it.

Now, here's what is going to happen. If it's not me in the position, it's one of these politicians that we're running against, you know, the 400 people that we're (inaudible). And here's what's going to happen.

They're not so stupid. They know it's not a good thing, and they may even be upset by it. But then they're going to get a call from the donors or probably from the lobbyist for Ford and say, "You can't do that to Ford, because Ford takes care of me and I take care of you, and you can't do that to Ford."

And guess what? No problem. They're going to build in Mexico. They're going to take away thousands of jobs. It's very bad for us.

So, under President Trump, here's what would happen:

The head of Ford will call me back, I would say within an hour after I told them the bad news. But it could be he'd want to be cool, and he'll wait until the next day. You know, they want to be a little cool.

And he'll say, "Please, please, please." He'll beg for a little while, and I'll say, "No interest." Then he'll call all sorts of political people, and I'll say, "Sorry, fellas. No interest," because I don't need anybody's money. It's nice. I don't need anybody's money.

I'm using my own money. I'm not using the lobbyists. I'm not using donors. I don't care. I'm really rich. I (inaudible).

And by the way, I'm not even saying that's the kind of mindset, that's the kind of thinking you need for this country.

So— because we got to make the country rich.

It sounds crass. Somebody said, "Oh, that's crass." It's not crass.

We got $18 trillion in debt. We got nothing but problems.

We got a military that needs equipment all over the place. We got nuclear weapons that are obsolete.

We've got nothing. We've got Social Security that's going to be destroyed if somebody like me doesn't bring money into the country. All these other people want to cut the hell out of it. I'm not going to cut it at all; I'm going to bring money in, and we're going to save it.

[The people got to see how smart Donald Trump is on real life and what a great businessman he is through these stories and more and more believed that he would get the job done for Americans if only he could get the politicians in the swamp out of the way. The people loved Trump's promise to drain the swamp, That, ladies and gentlemen is Why Trump Got Elected!]

But here's what's going to happen:

After I'm called by 30 friends of mine who contributed to different campaigns, after I'm called by all of the special interests and by the— the donors and by the lobbyists— and they have zero chance at convincing me, zero— I'll get a call the next day from the head of Ford. He'll say. "Please reconsider," I'll say no.
He'll say, "Mr. President, we've decided to move the plant back to the United States, and we're not going to build it in Mexico." That's it. They have no choice. They have no choice.

There are hundreds of things like that. I'll give you another example.

Saudi Arabia, they make $1 billion a day. $1 billion a day. I love the Saudis. Many are in this building. They make a billion dollars a day. Whenever they have problems, we send over the ships. We say "we're gonna protect." What are we doing? They've got nothing but money.

If the right person asked them, they'd pay a fortune. They wouldn't be there except for us.

And believe me, you look at the border with Yemen. You remember Obama a year ago, Yemen was a great victory. Two weeks later, the place was blown up. Everybody got out— and they kept our equipment.

They always keep our equipment. We ought to send used equipment, right? They always keep our equipment. We ought to send some real junk, because, frankly, it would be— we ought to send our surplus. We're always losing this gorgeous brand-new stuff.

But look at that border with Saudi Arabia. Do you really think that these people are interested in Yemen? Saudi Arabia without us is gone. They're gone.

And I'm the one that made all of the right predictions about Iraq. You know, all of these politicians that I'm running against now— it's so nice to say I'm running as opposed to if I run, if I run. I'm running.

But all of these politicians that I'm running against now, they're trying to disassociate. I mean, you looked at Bush, it took him five days to answer the question on Iraq. He couldn't answer the question. He didn't know. I said, "Is he intelligent?"

Then I looked at Rubio. He was unable to answer the question, is Iraq a good thing or bad thing? He didn't know. He couldn't answer the question.

How are these people gonna lead us? How are we gonna— how are we gonna go back and make it great again? We can't. They don't have a clue. They can't lead us. They can't. They can't even answer simple questions. It was terrible.

But Saudi Arabia is in big, big trouble. Now, thanks to fracking and other things, the oil is all over the place. And I used to say it, there are ships at sea, and this was during the worst crisis, that were loaded up with oil, and the cartel kept the price up, because, again, they were smarter than our leaders. They were smarter than our leaders.

There is so much wealth out there that can make our country so rich again, and therefore make it great again. Because we need money. We're dying. We're dying. We need money. We have to do it. And we need the right people.

So, Ford will come back. They'll all come back. And I will say this, this is going to be an election, in my opinion, that's based on competence.

Somebody said — thank you, darlin'.

Somebody said to me the other day, a reporter, a very nice reporter, "But, Mr. Trump, you're not a nice person."

That's true. But actually I am. I think I am a nice person. People that know me, like me. Does my family like me? I think so, right. Look at my family. I'm proud of my family.

By the way, speaking of my family, Melania, Barron, Kai, Donnie, Don, Vanessa, Tiffany, Ivanka did a great job. Did she do a great job?

Great. Jared, Laura and Eric, I'm very proud of my family. They're a great family.
So, the reporter said to me the other day, "But, Mr. Trump, you're not a nice person. How can you get people to vote for you?"

I said, "I don't know." I said, "I think that number one, I am a nice person. I give a lot of money away to charities and other things. I think I'm actually a very nice person."

But, I said, "This is going to be an election that's based on competence, because people are tired of these nice people. And they're tired of being ripped off by everybody in the world. And they're tired of spending more money on education than any nation in the world per capita, than any nation in the world, and we are 26th in the world, 25 countries are better than us in education. And some of them are like third world countries. But we're becoming a third world country, because of our infrastructure, our airports, our roads, everything."

So, one of the things I did, and I said, you know what I'll do. I'll do it. Because a lot of people said, "He'll never run. Number one, he won't want to give up his lifestyle."

They're right about that, but I'm doing it.

Number two, I'm a private company, so nobody knows what I'm worth. And the one thing is that when you run, you have to announce and certify to all sorts of governmental authorities your net worth.

So, I said, "That's OK." I'm proud of my net worth. I've done an amazing job.

I started off— thank you— I started off in a small office with my father in Brooklyn and Queens, and my father said — and I love my father. I learned so much. He was a great negotiator. I learned so much just sitting at his feet playing with blocks listening to him negotiate with subcontractors. But I learned a lot.

But he used to say, "Donald, don't go into Manhattan. That's the big leagues. We don't know anything about that. Don't do it."

I said, "I gotta go into Manhattan. I gotta build those big buildings. I gotta do it, Dad. I've gotta do it."

And after four or five years in Brooklyn, I ventured into Manhattan and did a lot of great deals— the Grand Hyatt Hotel. I was responsible for the convention center on the west side. I did a lot of great deals, and I did them early and young. And now I'm building all over the world, and I love what I'm doing.

But they all said, a lot of the pundits on television, "Well, Donald will never run, and one of the main reasons is he's private and he's probably not as successful as everybody thinks."

So, I said to myself, you know, nobody's ever going to know unless I run, because I'm really proud of my success. I really am.

I've employed— I've employed tens of thousands of people over my lifetime. That means medical. That means education. That means everything.

So, a large accounting firm and my accountants have been working for months, because it's big and complex, and they've put together a statement, a financial statement, just a summary. But everything will be filed eventually with the government, and we don't [use] extensions or anything. We'll be filing it right on time. We don't need anything.

And it was even reported incorrectly yesterday, because they said, "He had assets of $9 billion." So, I said, "No, that's the wrong number. That's the wrong number. Not assets."

So, they put together this. And before I say it, I have to say this. I made it the old-fashioned way. It's real estate. You know, it's real estate.

It's labor, and it's unions—good and some bad—and lots of people that aren't in unions, and it's all over the place and building all over the world.

And I have assets— big accounting firm, one of the most highly respected— 9 billion 240 million dollars.

And I have liabilities of about $500 million. That's long-term debt, very low interest rates.

In fact, one of the big banks came to me and said, "Donald, you don't have enough borrowings. Could we loan you $4 billion"? I said, "I don't need it. I don't want it. And I've been there. I don't want it."

But in two seconds, they give me whatever I wanted. So I have a total net worth, and now with the increase, it'll be well-over $10 billion. But here, a total net worth of—net worth, not assets, not— a net worth, after all debt, after all expenses, the greatest assets— Trump Tower, 1290 Avenue of the Americas, Bank of America building in San Francisco, 40 Wall Street, sometimes referred to as the Trump building right opposite the New York— many other places all over the world.

So the total is $8,737,540,00.

Now I'm not doing that...

I'm not doing that to brag, because you know what? I don't have to brag. I don't have to, believe it or not.

I'm doing that to say that that's the kind of thinking our country needs. We need that thinking. We have the opposite thinking.

We have losers. We have losers. We have people that don't have it. We have people that are morally corrupt. We have people that are selling this country down the drain.

So, I put together this statement, and the only reason I'm telling you about it today is because we really do have to get going, because if we have another three or four years— you know, we're at $8 trillion now. We're soon going to be at $20 trillion.

According to the economists— who I'm not big believers in, but, nevertheless, this is what they're saying— that $24 trillion— we're very close— that's the point of no return. $24 trillion. We will be there soon. That's when we become Greece. That's when we become a country that's unsalvageable. And we're gonna be there very soon. We're gonna be there very soon.

So, just to sum up, I would do various things very quickly. I would repeal and replace the big lie, Obamacare.

I would build a great wall, and nobody builds walls better than me, believe me, and I'll build them very inexpensively, I will build a great, great wall on our southern border. And I will have Mexico pay for that wall.

Mark my words.

Nobody would be tougher on ISIS than Donald Trump. Nobody.

I will find — within our military, I will find the General Patton, or I will find General MacArthur, I will find the right guy. I will find the guy that's going to take that military and make it really work. Nobody, nobody will be pushing us around.

I will stop Iran from getting nuclear weapons. And we won't be using a man like Secretary Kerry that has absolutely no concept of negotiation, who's making a horrible and laughable deal, who's just being tapped along as they make weapons right now, and then goes into a bicycle race at 72 years old, and falls and breaks his leg. I won't be doing that. And I promise I will never be in a bicycle race. That I can tell you.

I will immediately terminate President Obama's illegal executive order on immigration, immediately.

Fully support and back up the Second Amendment.

Now, it's very interesting. Today I heard it. Through stupidity, in a very, very hard-core prison, interestingly named Clinton, two vicious murderers, two vicious people escaped, and nobody knows where they are. And a woman was on television this morning, and she said, "You know, Mr. Trump," and she was telling other people, and I actually called her, and she said, "You know, Mr. Trump, I always was against guns. I didn't want guns. And now since this happened"— it's up in the prison area— "my husband and I are finally in agreement, because he wanted the guns. We now have a gun on every table. We're ready to start shooting."

I said, "Very interesting."

So, protect the Second Amendment.

End— end Common Core. Common Core should— it is a disaster. Bush is totally in favor of Common Core. I don't see how he can possibly get the nomination. He's weak on immigration. He's in favor of Common Core. How the hell can you vote for this guy? You just can't do it. We have to end education -- has to be local.

Rebuild the country's infrastructure.

Nobody can do that like me. Believe me. It will be done on time, on budget, way below cost, way below what anyone ever thought.

I look at the roads being built all over the country, and I say I can build those things for one-third. What they do is unbelievable, how bad.

You know, we're building on Pennsylvania Avenue, the Old Post Office, we're converting it into one of the world's great hotels. It's gonna be the best hotel in Washington, D.C. We got it from the General Services Administration in Washington. The Obama administration. We got it. It was the most highly sought after— or one of them, but I think the most highly sought-after project in the history of General Services. We got it. People were shocked, Trump got it.

Well, I got it for two reasons. Number one, we're really good. Number two, we had a really good plan. And I'll add in the third, we had a great financial statement. Because the General Services, who are terrific people, by the way, and talented people, they wanted to do a great job. And they wanted to make sure it got built.

So, we have to rebuild our infrastructure, our bridges, our roadways, our airports. You come into La Guardia Airport, it's like we're in a third world country. You look at the patches and the 40-year-old floor. They throw down asphalt, and they throw.

You look at these airports, we are like a third world country. And I come in from China and I come in from Qatar and I come in from different places, and they have the most incredible airports in the world. You come to back to this country and you have LAX, disaster. You have all of these disastrous airports. We have to rebuild our infrastructure.

Save Medicare, Medicaid and Social Security without cuts. Have to do it.

Get rid of the fraud. Get rid of the waste and abuse, but save it. People have been paying it for years. And now many of these candidates want to cut it. You save it by making the United States, by making us rich again, by taking back all of the money that's being lost.

Renegotiate our foreign trade deals.

Reduce our $18 trillion in debt, because, believe me, we're in a bubble. We have artificially low interest rates. We have a stock market that, frankly, has been good to me, but I still hate to see what's happening. We have a stock market that is so bloated.

Be careful of a bubble because what you've seen in the past might be small potatoes compared to what happens. So be very, very careful.

And strengthen our military and take care of our vets. So, so important.

Sadly, the American dream is dead.

But if I get elected president I will bring it back bigger and better and stronger than ever before, and we will make America great again.

Thank you. Thank you very much.

So, in this speech, Donald Trump showed that he was no dummy. Furthermore, he spoke American, not politician to the many Americans who had been hearing politician-speak for far too many years. Donald Trump gave this speech and over 300-others like it and his tone never changed. Donald Trump loves America and all Americans who love America love that Donald Trump loves America. That's "Why Donald Trump Got Elected."

Chapter 9 Why Did Anybody Vote For Trump?

Americans could not take our country for granted

From the eyes of many, for eight years of Obama running the ship without a license, the United States was in imminent danger and we needed a comprehensive, yet workable solution to bring us back on the right economic track. America needed to be infused with a positive sense of the future so that even before the Tax Reform in December 2017, we would know things were getting so good that we could put the *Apply Inside* signs back outside. It's getting better every day. That's "Why Trump Was Elected President!"

The reason there have been no real middle-class jobs for most of the Obama years, was because the economy was caput. It was not working. Why was it not working? How about not having one businessman on the former president's cabinet to help right the big ship US. It was as if the former president was trying to assure failure.

The prior administration was ideologically driven, and its policies and regulations had made businesses afraid to invest in America. The government was perceived as the chief causative problem for the malaise. Instead of government wanting to help, those in the know, companies were asking for government to please get out of the way.

But, in eight years, the official US would not get out of the way. Instead, it injected itself where it could do the most harm. Some saw their lack of support for America as "that's all she wrote for the country!" Government philosophies had to change for America to have a chance. Donald Trump was perceived as a breath of fresh air. He was what had been missing—a leader who would paint it all fresh with a new paint brush and great paint to boot—the best paint you could get!

One way to change government philosophies of course, would be for the same people, who created the problem, to change their ways. That rarely happens. Another way to change government philosophies is to change governments. We get to do that at the federal level every two to six years with representatives. Once every four years, we get to change Presidents.

This time, the people decided that the presidency should be handed off to the person that had great prospects for success. I speak of Donald J. Trump, who is now our CEO, whether he is liked or unliked by an unkind press. Americans in 30 of 50 states chose Donald J. Trump and most of us are very pleased that we no longer have to go to a swamp of corruption to hope to move the country forward.

The reason "Why Trump Got Elected!" is because from everything that was out there, only Trump had the guts to fire all the officials who had given up America for Obama. Only Trump could and only Trump wanted to save America for *We the People* and for those who will live long after us.

I continually thank Mr. Trump for running. He is a tough, brave man. Historians will say that he had lots of other things that he could have done with his time.

Great things sometimes come in email

Like you, I have received many things in email without attribution. Many, I wanted to believe so much that I passed them on without checking anywhere. I do not particularly like Snopes as it almost always, from my observations, gives the liberal socialist progressive viewpoint like as if a Democrat activist did the analysis, and wrote an anti-American thesis about it.

Rarely does Snopes call anything correctly. Things that are very believable are declared false without what I consider a proper explanation. Nonetheless, I use Snopes myself as a conservative Democrat to see what the other side thinks about given matters. Don't count on Snopes for the unbiased truth. In fact, most fact checkers are getting checks from various wings of the Democratic Party for being fine foot soldiers.

By the way, in addition to email, I also found a written piece on https://reclaimourrepublic.wordpress.com. The full URL is https://reclaimourrepublic.wordpress.com/2016/06/02/video-honestly-why-would-anyone-vote-for-trump-press-covers-trump-inaccurately/

Right on the first page of this URL is a picture of this beautiful lady shown for your review on the next page. Just looking at this wonderful picture (seen in color on the Kindle version of this book), would be enough for me to reevaluate my posture on Donald Trump if I did not already know how great he was about to be. And, unlike Obama, a faux great, Trump has proven himself as a great man while on his mission to save America.

My whole extended family and I love the fact that Donald Trump is now our President and we wish him and his family well in this most arduous task. I thank Fred L. Anderson for this great email. It was proudly signed Fred L. Anderson. I could not find it on Snopes, which I believe means that Snopes could find no material to denigrate the piece or the author.

The email is printed on the next pages as received with emphasis asterisks removed. The paragraph immediately below, preceding the email, is from a retired lawyer. I adjusted it very slightly to mute a few words that might first appear objectionable. The essence of what was said is still in the paragraph on the next page.

VIDEO Honestly, Why Would Anyone Vote For Trump? – Press covers Trump inaccurately

Posted on June 2, 2016

Believing fervently that anyone in the phone book would make a better president than either the disgusting creature whom the Dems will nominate or the guy who many liberals think is a narcissistic empty suit, I am trying to see Trump in a better light than that cast by the parrots collectively comprising the national media. I found the attached piece, sent to me by a Naples, Florida, retiree, encouraging in that regard, and would commend it to your attention.

Here is the rest of the Email/Article:

Honestly, Why you should vote for Trump? — Press covers Trump inaccurately

A few days ago someone -- I don't know who, asked this question ... and a mutual friend (knowing I am a Trump supporter), tagged me and asked me to answer the question. Here is my reply from during the heat of the campaign.

[This is an answer to "Why Trump Got Elected!"]

I am a Trump supporter for several reasons. I believe that our country is at a critical tipping point and we don't have another presidential term to figure this out.

Health care costs are out of control, our labor participation rate is at a 50-year low, we have no borders, jobs are leaving by the thousands, the debt service on our national debt is nearing a point where we simply cannot pay it.

The average person hasn't had an increase in pay in 12 years. Over half the black men in our country are out of work. We are more divided than I can ever remember and I'm over 60 years old. We are at the brink of losing our country.

On top of that we spend money we don't have fighting wars we shouldn't be in, and cannot win. We pay over a hundred other countries billions of dollars a year and our military are the policemen for the world. We must fix this mess ASAP.

Now, before I give you my reasons, I need to share my perspective. I am an evangelical Christian. but I don't believe it is the role of government to legislate morality. I am a service connected disabled veteran having served in the US Army as a paratrooper.

I started my second career as an auto mechanic and worked my way up to owning 12 auto repair franchises. I then sold them and began a new career in real estate, building my own company to over 150 agents.

Then in 2003 I invented a technology that put me on CNN and I began selling that software to real estate agents internationally. I've written 14 books, thousands of trade articles and have trained over 1,000,000 real estate agents in specific professional skills.

I've employed over a thousand people during that time, and until a month ago have been a registered democrat. Okay, now that you know where I'm coming from, here are my reasons:

First, his resume. Of everyone running for president, Trump is the only one who has ever employed anyone. He is the only one who has any experience in international trade. He is the only one who understands the impact of our tax laws and government regulation on companies and jobs.

Trump has made a fortune turning around failed companies. He's worked complicated deals all over the world, negotiating with governments, labor unions, and international financiers. These skills are not learned overnight and we don't have time for another life-long politician and attorney to get up to speed.

Second is his character. He is tough as nails. His children are pretty awesome. You can tell a lot about somebody by their kids. He is brutally honest as opposed to being politically correct. His employees and his ex-employees have nothing but praise for him. Even his ex-wives have nothing bad to say about him. Check it out.

Third is his success. He has built hundreds of successful businesses. One of his companies declared bankruptcy (chapter 11 or reorganization) four separate times before ultimately saving the company. All creditors were paid, and jobs were saved. Bottom line is he is just a very good businessman.

Fourth is that he is a great negotiator. In fact, he wrote the book on negotiation -- The Art of the Deal, an international best-seller. If we are to save this country, we need someone who can work with people of differing opinions. Congress is grid locked. We need to work new trade agreements with other nations. We need to renegotiate treaties.

Fifth, Trump is a nationalist and not a globalist. He believes that our country comes first. We need to enforce our borders and the rule of law. He believes it is not our job to defend the whole world. He believes that if we do help countries with their defense, we should be paid for it.

Sixth, he has great instincts. He predicted the rise of Osama bin Laden. He predicted a terror attack on a major US city. He opposed the war in Iraq although every other candidate, but Bernie Sanders was in favor of the war. He opposed it because it would destabilize the Middle East. He got out of the gaming industry before it crashed. Great instincts.

Seventh, he is a natural leader. Even those who don't like him are following his lead. He has single-handedly set the agenda for this election cycle. He is respected internationally as well as in our nation. He oozes leadership.

Eighth, he is a great communicator and persuader. He is a master at using the media to advance his narrative. He totally understands the media. He built the most successful reality show in the history of television. These are skills he will need if he is to turn this country around.

Ninth, I have studied him. I read his first book in 1987 and realized he was a brilliant businessman. I've watched hundreds of hours of speeches, media interviews, read thousands of articles about him, several of his books, and studied his successes and his failures. He is the real deal. I challenge anyone to study him and not support him.

Finally, I have to look at what motivates him. Most politicians are motivated by money and/or power. Trump already has both. He has a history of being a patriot, from his military high school, to now. He has a huge ego, like every other candidate running. The difference is he is honest about his.

I think he sees our nation at a critical place and he knows that he has the unique skill set to fix the problems. If he does, he will go down in history as being one of the greatest presidents ever.

If you understand him, you know that his legacy is important to him (his name on all his buildings and companies). I even believe he is funding his own campaign, so he won't owe favors or loyalties to special interests. When you evaluate his motivations, you can't help but admire him.

I remembered one more reason. Everyone is about to blow a gasket over him. The establishment Republican Party hates him and has actually been actively trying to take down their own front runner. The establishment Democrat Party hates him because they know he will crush Hillary in the election, and the establishment media hates him because he totally controls the news cycle and they cannot control him. Even the donor class hates him because he cannot be bought. If all these people who I cannot stand, hate him, that only makes me love him more.

You know who loves him? The regular people in this country. The ones who work their asses off every day and haven't had a pay raise in over a decade. The ones who pay the taxes and watch as their jobs get shipped overseas or across the border. The ones who see their property values going down because corrupt Big Banking blew up the housing market. The ones whose retirement is in jeopardy because social security has been raided and their 401Ks have been decimated by corrupt Wall Street.

Think about this: We've had politicians running our country for way too many years and look at the results. Isn't it time we give a business person the opportunity to show the way a country should be run.....like a business, because that's what our country is!*

Fred L Anderson

-----Fred, this is Brian, also in my sixties... I agree... Thank you for writing this to all of America!

Chapter 10 Trump's J. Q. Public Political Platform

This could have been written by John Q. Public himself.

The person who sent me this email, my good friend Eppy Harding, surely loves me as this email is very insightful. It is yet another great email, which provides valuable sagacity into how Donald J. Trump is expected to serve as our president. I received this set of platform points unattributed to the original author in February 2016 while the primary campaign was firing up. It has all the issues identified. It is another great read.

Some of these notions have been previously rendered in this book. The mystery writer was unaware that we would be highlighting the works of others. Some of these notions are worth hearing again.

Read your email for insights

Trump's posture on these issues is "Why Trump Got Elected!"

I checked out the email as best I could and sent it on to my other email friends. I have reproduced it in its entirety for your reading pleasure and edification. I hope you enjoy it below. Donald Trump is quite a guy, and this is his platform as deduced from his writings and speeches by the unknown email writer. Now that he is president, we have a right to expect great things.

Date: 2/29/2016 11:01:38 A.M. Eastern Standard Time
Subj: FW: Trump
Sent: Sunday, February 28, 2016 5:32 PM
Subject: Trump

THIS IS DONALD TRUMP'S POLITICAL PLATFORM

1.) Trump believes that America should not intervene militarily in other country's problems without being compensated for doing so. If America is going to risk the lives of our soldiers and incur the expense of going to war, then the nations we help must be willing to pay for our help.

Using the Iraq War as an example, he cites the huge monetary expense to American taxpayers (over $1.5 trillion, and possibly much more depending on what sources are used to determine the cost) in addition to the cost in human life. He suggests that Iraq should have been required to give us enough of their oil to pay for the expenses we incurred.

He includes in those expenses the medical costs for our military and $5 million for each family that lost a loved one in the war and $2 million for each family of soldiers who received severe injuries.

2.) Speaking of the military, Trump wants America to have a strong military again. He believes the single most important function of the federal government is national defense. He has said he wants to find the General Patton or General MacArthur that could lead our military buildup back to the strength it needs to be. [Mad Dog Mattis fits the bill so far.]

While he hasn't said it directly that I know of, Trump's attitude about America and about winning tells me he'd most likely be quick to eliminate rules of engagement that handicap our military in battle. Clearly Trump is a "win at all costs" kind of guy, and I'm sure that would apply to our national defense and security, too.

3.) Trump wants a strong foreign policy and believes that it must include 7 core principles:

✓ American interests come first. Always. No apologies.
✓ Maximum firepower and military preparedness.
✓ Only go to war to win.
✓ Stay loyal to your friends and suspicious of your enemies.
✓ Keep the technological sword razor sharp.
✓ See the unseen. Prepare for threats before they materialize.
✓ Respect and support our present and past warriors.

4.) Trump believes that terrorists who are captured should be treated as military combatants, not as criminals like the Obama administration treats them.

5.) Trump makes the point that China's manipulation of their currency has given them unfair advantage in our trade dealings with them. He says we must tax their imports to offset their currency manipulation, which will cause American companies to be competitive again and drive manufacturing back to America and create jobs here.

Although he sees China as the biggest offender, he believes that America should protect itself from all foreign efforts to take our jobs and manufacturing. For example, Ford is building a plant in Mexico and Trump suggests that every part or vehicle Ford makes in Mexico be taxed 35% if they want to bring it into the U. S., which would cause companies like Ford to no longer be competitive using their Mexican operations and move manufacturing back to the U. S., once again creating jobs here.

6.) Trump wants passage of NOPEC legislation (No Oil Producing and Exporting Cartels Act NOPEC S.394), which would allow the government to sue OPEC for violating antitrust laws. According to Trump, that would break up the cartel. He also wants to unleash our energy companies to drill domestically thereby increasing domestic production creating jobs and driving domestic costs of oil and gas down while reducing dependence on foreign oil.

7.) Trump believes a secure border is critical for both security and prosperity in America. He wants to build a wall to stop illegals from entering. He wants to put real controls on immigration. (And he says he'll get Mexico to pay for the wall, which many have scoffed at, but given his business successes I wouldn't put it past him.) He also wants to enforce our immigration laws and provide no path to citizenship for illegals.

8.) Trump wants a radical change to the tax system to not only make it better for average Americans, but also to encourage businesses to stay here and foreign businesses to move here. [The first step was the Tax Bill passed in December 2017] The resulting influx of money to our nation would do wonders for our economy. He wants to make America the place to do business.

He also wants to lower the death tax and the taxes on capital gains and dividends. This would put more than $1.6 trillion back into the economy and help rebuild the 1.5 million jobs we've lost to the current tax system. He also wants to charge companies who outsource jobs overseas a 20% tax, but for those willing to move jobs back to America they would not be taxed. And for citizens he has a tax plan that would allow Americans to keep more of what they earn and spark economic growth. He wants to change the personal income tax to:

> Up to $30,000 taxed at 1%
> From $30,000 to $100,000 taxed at 5%
> From $100,000 to $1,000,000 taxed at 10%
> $1,000,000 and above taxed at 15%

9.) Trump wants Obamacare repealed. He says it's a "job-killing, health care-destroying monstrosity that can't be reformed, salvaged, or fixed." He believes in allowing real competition in the health insurance marketplace to allow competition to drive prices down. He also believes in tort reform to get rid of defensive medicine and lower costs.

10.) Trump wants spending reforms in Washington, acknowledging that America spends far more than it receives in revenue. He has said he believes that if we don't stop increasing the national debt once it hits $24 trillion it will be impossible to save this country.

11.) Even though he says we need to cut spending, he does not want to harm those on Medicare, Medicaid, or Social Security. He believes that the citizens have faithfully paid in to the system to have these services available and that the American government has an obligation to fulfill its end of the bargain and provide those benefits. Therefore, he wants to build the economy up so that we have the revenue to pay those costs without cutting the benefits to the recipients.

He disagrees with Democrats who think raising taxes is the answer and says that when you do that you stifle the economy. On the other hand, when you lower taxes and create an environment to help businesses they will grow, hire more workers, and those new workers will be paying taxes that becomes more tax revenue for the government.

12.) Trump also wants reform of the welfare state saying that America needs "a safety net, not a hammock." He believes in a welfare to work program that would help reduce the welfare rolls, and encourage people to get back to work. And he wants a crackdown on entitlement fraud. [My way of saying this is that Trump wants to help the helpless, but he does not want to help make people helpless.]

13.) Trump believes climate change is a hoax. {emails that were hacked prove they are lying to benefit their ideological agenda]

14.) Trump opposes Common Core [Notion that Education should be controlled by Feds].

15.) Trump is pro-life, although he allows for an exception due to rape, incest, or the life of the mother.

16.) Trump is pro 2nd Amendment rights.

17.) Trump's view on same-sex marriage is that marriage is between a man and a woman, but he also believes that this is a states' rights issue, not a federal issue.

18.) Trump supports the death penalty. Trump believes that there is a lack of common sense, innovative thinking in Washington [(Hmmm looks like he believes in horse sense!] He says it's about seeing the unseen and that's the kind of thinking we need to turn this country around. He tells a personal story to illustrate the point:

"When I opened Trump National Golf Club at Rancho Palos Verdes in Los Angeles, I was immediately told that I would need to build a new and costly ballroom. The current ballroom was gorgeous, but it only sat 200 people and we were losing business because people needed a larger space for their events.

Building a new ballroom would take years to get approval and permits (since it's on the Pacific Ocean), and cost about $5 million. I took one look at the ballroom and saw immediately what needed to be done. The problem wasn't the size of the room, it was the size of the chairs.

They were huge, heavy, and unwieldy. We didn't need a bigger ballroom, we needed smaller chairs! So, I had them replaced with high-end, smaller chairs. I then had our people sell the old chairs and got more money for them than the cost of the new chairs. In the end, the ballroom went from seating 200 people to seating 320 people.

Our visitors got the space they desired, and I spared everyone the hassle of years of construction and $5 million of expense. It's amazing what you can accomplish with a little common sense."

End of email----

On top of his saving years of construction and $5 million in expenses, he also was able to keep the ballroom open for business during the time it would have been under remodeling, which allowed him to continue to make money on the space instead of losing that revenue during construction time.

Donald Trump's entire life has been made up of success and winning. He's been accused of bankruptcies, but that's not true. He's never filed personal bankruptcy. He's bought companies and legally used bankruptcy laws to restructure their debt, just as businesses do all the time. But he's never been bankrupt personally.

He's a fighter that clearly loves America and would fight for our nation.

Trump says, "I love America. And when you love something, you protect it passionately - fiercely, even." We never hear that from Democrats or even from most Republicans. Donald Trump is saying things that desperately need to be said but no other candidate has shown the fortitude to stand up and say them.

Looking over this list of what he wants for America I see a very necessary set of goals that are long past due. Before we criticize someone because the media does, maybe we should seriously consider what the person has to offer.

(Most of the information on Trump's positions and plans for America come from his 2011 book, *Time to Get Tough*)

Because this is who Donald Trump really is, his supporters know that this is "Why Trump Got Elected!"

Chapter 11 Veterans Love Donald Trump

Trump loves the Veterans

The Veterans of America have not been convinced by Democratic mumbo-jumbo that Obama should have been crowned emperor. They saw how the US prosecuted wars under Obama and why we looked like a Banana Republic at the top while our honorable fighting men received rules of engagement that created more American deaths and casualties in foreign wars than necessary. Obama ran the wars like he was on his personal iPhone and the men in uniform were manipulable pawns. You can't fool US veterans even some of the time.

Moreover, the problems with people dying, who had been waiting for care in Veterans Hospitals is inexcusable. Obama never made it a priority to solve this big problem at VA Hospitals across the US. Ask friends you know who work in the VA. It has been one of Trump's top priorities from his entry into the race. For Veterans of the US Military, and there are many of them with a lot of big families, that is "Why Trump Got Elected!"

Donald Trump was ready to talk about Veterans issues at a Veterans event during his campaign. His plan had been to jump right in and begin his speech about what he would do to reform Veterans Affairs (VA). Instead, he knew military people understood the power of guns in the hands of good guys, So, he brought up the attack on the police in Dallas from the prior week. You may recall that five police officers were murdered during an anti-police street protest.

To bring you back up to date on that situation, there was a heavily armed sniper who gunned down police officers in downtown Dallas. This brutal attack left five of them dead. This was no accident. The sniper specifically set out to kill as many white officers as he could. It was not ISIS, it was clearly misguided black v white. He was a military veteran who had served in Afghanistan. He had a major arsenal in his home that included ammunition and enough bomb-making materials to wipe out a large number of citizens.

This event was to be a demonstration against the fatal police shootings of black men in Minnesota and Louisiana and the march was intended to be peaceful. It was focused on violence committed by police officers who were in a scene of chaos and bloodshed aimed against them. But, instead the police were summarily mowed down.

The sniper shooting thus was the type of retaliatory violence that many people have feared from two years of protests about black shootings and deaths such as Freddy Gray around the country. President Obama always sided against law enforcement. This forced yet another wrenching shift in debates over race and criminal justice that already had our nation deeply divided. In the streets, many in the white community believed that these shootings of officers had to do with Obama and Mrs. Clinton favoring the criminals over the police. It was not white or black. It was politics.

"Our police officers run into danger every single day," but often are "under relentless criticism," Trump stated, as he defended law enforcement. "I want our nation's police to know that we thank you from the bottom of our heart... we support you and we will always stand with you." Trump vowed to the police, adding that after the attack in Dallas, "Our whole nation is in mourning." We sure are but we can do lots better to assure safety and peace than by forcing the DOJ on local departments. Trump has already stopped that without legislation.

Trump explained that "Law enforcement separates civilization from total chaos...The police are needed the most where crime is the highest." It is only a matter of black and white if the President and Hillary and Loretta Lynch say it is. Most normal Americans, white and black alike, find crime reprehensible and are pleased that the police find the bad guys, again, white or black, and they put the bad guys away because they are bad guys.

During the election time, Barack Obama and Hillary Clinton had been sending signals that favor the criminal element over law enforcement. They wanted to release criminals, who would become Democratic voters, so that officers had to arrest them again—but only after they voted. And, thus there is no question that Donald Trump was the Law and Order Candidate. The people saw through the ruse of the Democrats and that is "Why Trump Got Elected!"

When talking to the veterans, Trump compared the backlash that police are facing across the country to the backlash Vietnam veterans faced in the past, saying, "For too many police today, that is their daily reality." He then went on to call veterans a group who "represent the very best of America. He noted that he intended to keep all his promises to veterans including their protection. "You defend America and America will defend you." But that promise even this early in the Trump Administration has been broken by our politicians, who forget too soon who elected them.

"Hillary Clinton during the campaign said of the VA scandal that it has not been as wide spread as it has been made out to be...she's been part of this rigged system for a long time. Perhaps it' has been easy in the past for politicians to lose touch with reality as they have lost touch with real people. The disconnect in America is very deep. There are two Americas: the ruling class and the groups that it favors, and then everyone else."

The Veterans were moved by Donald Trump's words and his sincerity. It was like moving from a nasty cartoon world into a video of how life could be in America with positive leadership.

Trump offered to the veterans that if elected, he would conduct an investigation immediately that would reveal even more corruption within the VA. "Fixing this corruption will be one of my many and highest priorities. Trump, now is the president and he is keeping his promise as the veterans knew that he would.

"Every Veteran will get timely access to top quality medical care," Trump promised that Veterans will have "the right to choose their doctor and clinics... "We must extend this right to all veterans," Mr. Trump stressed.

Clearly, I have been a Trump supporter from day one and I am glad that Donald Trump is now making good on keeping his promises with Veterans and with Law Enforcement Departments across the country. He is to be our next president for seven more years.

As a Democrat, I watch my party closely and it has gotten disgusting that there is no high ground for the Dem leadership. I felt that four years of a Hillary Clinton presidency would be just enough to kill our country. So, did the Veterans who in unison, voted for Donald Trump, with big smiles on their faces. That's "Why Trump Got Elected!"

The Democratic Party is so far left and for whatever reason, so anti-white today that I prayed during the general election that mostly all Democrats would be defeated in November. We tried anti-white with Obama for eight years. He was supposedly the first post-racial president and it has only gotten worse and it is simply because of poor leadership all around.

During his meeting with Veterans, Donald Trump described himself as "a law-and-order Republican running against a weak and ineffective Democrat, who can't be trusted to keep America safe." I do believe this as I have seen it.

Mr. Trump chose not to address head on the topic of race as he condemned critics of law enforcement in a carefully worded speech that protested police shootings of African Americans. Police shootings simply are wrong. But the topic of race cannot be broached single-handedly as the corrupt media would use it against Mr. Trump for the benefit of their Democrat agenda. Yet, the problem cannot be solved without addressing the root cause.

Nobody wants this. Nobody wants what is going on between blacks and whites and between blacks and police. It may help to know that Americans generally overestimate, to a significant degree, the percentage of the U.S. population that is either black or Hispanic. According to the U.S. Census Bureau, 12.3% of the U.S. population is black, and 12.5% is Hispanic. Additionally, it is recorded that 12% of the police population is black.

Thus, it appears that the black police population matches the black percentage overall. Consequently, the notion of black people killing police officers because they are police simply does not make sense.

Intrinsically, we know that all lives matter, period. I happen to be white and I know my life matters to me as do the lives of my family and my friends, some of whom are black. I know that black lives matter as do brown lives and the lives of those of all people of all colors and creeds. And of course, blue lives matter because they are people too, and without them, lawlessness would reign supreme. Thank you for your police service.

So, let me repeat, nobody wants what is going on between blacks and whites and between blacks and the police. But it cannot be made better until all of us decide that it is worth it. Until we decide that, I fear Americans in the near future will be taking sides and the conflict will get even worse.

I am pleased that Donald Trump has been representing blacks and whites and other "races" in America by supporting the Veterans and the police. Trump is a truth-teller and when he calls a murder, a murder, he makes sure that we all know that all lives matter.

Murder is wrong no matter who gets murdered. Black, police, or white, or other. If we can convince the race baiters such as Jesse Jackson and Al Sharpton to join other black reverends and white reverends and police commissioners, and all come up with a way to tone down the rhetoric instead of creating a Hatfield and McCoy battle among the races and the police that will never end, we do have a chance. We have to want that chance and when we look at the corrupt press, it surely appears that they are not willing to give us that chance.

We should begin again what we thought we had done when mostly white people elected President Obama to lead our country. None of us expected to get racial strife out of that deal. We can do much better.

Hopefully our leaders from the new president to the new candidates to the reverends must get together now, as soon as possible—thinking of a solution regardless of what went on in the campaigns.

We need to mute the corrupt press or ignore their seditious message before they convince us to kill each other. It won't happen when contrived fake-news about one party or another being in league with the Russians is the news every day. We should no longer hold the seditious press in high regard. They serve against the people, not as the Fourth Estate.

Additionally, I would advise the president and the candidates to not make remarks that favor one race over another or which favor criminals over the police. Let this thing calm down.

Meanwhile campaigns and elections must go on. This 2016 campaign and election is over and let's acknowledge it. Baby faced Democrats and the bigger babies in the press won't let this past election become done. It is up to the people.

Donald Trump is our president. Donald Trump is president of all America. Nobody should boycott the State of the Union address whether an Barack Obama type or a Donald Trump type is the duly elected president. What does that help?

NJ Gov. Chris Christie, a former prosecutor, also took his shots during this period while praising law enforcement: "We need a president who will once again put law and order at the top of the priority of the presidency in this country... "Our police officers, the men and women who stand each day to protect us need to understand that the president of the united states and his administration will give them the benefit of the doubt, not always believe that what they've done is somehow wrong."

Donald Trump is that President and again, he supports all of America.

Chapter 12 Ben Carson, Friend of Donald Trump

Donlin Long and Ben Carson speak at Johns Hopkins Hospital in Baltimore after the surgery that separated conjoined twins in September 1987. (Fred Kraft/AP)

Ben Carson is a great man

During the RNC presidential primaries, a pleasant surprise for many nationalists and populists and conservatives was to see one of the most respected surgeons in the world, who had just run for the presidency and stepped down in favor of Donald Trump. This world-renowned physician / surgeon, who for years was on the prestigious John Hopkins Team, had pioneered the separation of conjoined "Siamese" twins with both twins living after the operation.

Though very famous for his accomplishments, because he is a conservative and not of the thinking of the mainstream press, their coverage after he ran for office was always negative. They feared a great black man might ruin the Obama legacy of coming from nowhere to ruin America.

They feared that Carson would come from nowhere, lift himself up by hiss bootstraps, become one of the most prestigious surgeons in America, run for President, and win. You see, though Obama was just ½ black, Carson was 100% black and so the truth on him could not be told. Neither the press, nor the Democratic Party wanted any normal US citizen to think that if a person was not a liberal Marxist progressive, who worshipped the legacy of Obama by name, whether they were white or black did not matter, they were like the anti-Christ. None of the people that broadcast such dribble were worthy of shining Ben Carson's shoes

Carson is the real deal. He was not and is not an egotist as his mom had taught him better while raising a family of American patriots. Nonetheless the American white dominated press decided to sacrifice a fine black man because he did not espouse their values of laziness and dependence on government to get ahead. Nonetheless, Carson cared deeply about an America that he was concerned would no longer give Americans the opportunities that he had when growing up and so when he was destroyed by the Democratic Party, he aligned himself with Donald Trump because their values were more similar than those who wished ill on America.

Ben Carson has never been a race-card player. After he withdrew from the presidential primary with very good showings, he found enough goodness in Donald Trump, as a black man, to support Trump's efforts to become the president of the United States. More books should be written about Ben Carson as he truly is an American hero.

Ben Carson today is the Housing and Urban Development (HUD) Secretary where he serves with distinction in the Trump Administration. Like the President, Dr. Carson takes nothing from the naysayers who want all Trump decisions to appear to be bad, that he is running the agency to help all those who are in need of housing. With his humble upbringing, brilliance as a human being, and great success in life, Ben Carson is the perfect HUD Secretary to work with the poor of all races to give them a better life. When helping people, Dr. Carson is 100% color blind.

For all of us, reading about Ben Carson is a treat. He is a very sincere man. Donald Trump asked him to speak at the RNC convention because he saw what we see in Ben Carson and was honored when Carson accepted. Dr. Ben Carson gave a powerful speech on Tuesday of Convention week, helping set the stage for Mr. Trump's ultimate triumph in the election. In the spirit of the title of this book, that is "Why Trump Got Elected!"

As good as his speech was for America, it did not stop the press from slamming a black man they do not like, simply because he really wanted to help all black men as he helps all men.

His speech on Tuesday night was electrifying. Here it is:

Ben Carson RNC Speech on Convention Tuesday

Before his speech, Carson called for Republicans to put aside their differences and focus on one thing: winning the election. In an interview with The Tennessean, Carson was unequivocal in his drive to see the bigger picture:

My main thought is that we've got to get people to understand what the stakes are in this election so that they can put their petty differences behind them and concentrate on making sure that we win because the consequences of not winning are not four or eight years of Hillary Clinton.

Carson also struck a sympathetic tone towards accusations that
Melania Trump copied parts of Michelle Obama's speech at the 2008
Democratic National Convention, saying that if Melania did indeed
lift from the First Lady, she did so based on "shared values" that
transcend party lines.

We present the full transcript of Dr. Carson's speech here because he
is one of a kind. For a man as special as Ben Carson to find some
sense of specialness in Donald Trump is something that all
Americans paid attention to. This speech is another reason "Why
Trump Won the Election!"

Here he goes at the convention:

Thank you, thank you, thank you everyone.

I want to thank you all for that very warm welcome. I have to start
out by saying one very important thing: I'm not politically correct.
And I hate political correctness because it's antithetical to the
founding principles of this country and the secular progressives use it

to make people sit down and shut up while they change everything. It's time for us to stand up and shout out about what we believe in.

You know, I devoted my career to studying and operating on the human brain. This remarkable organ defines our humanity. It gives us the ability to not only feel and observe, but to reason. When we elect a president, we need to use that power of reasoning to look at their history, their character, what kind of people they really are. It's all the difference in the world for us.

And it is gonna be so critical right now. We must resist the temptation to take the easy way out and to passively accept what is fed to us by the political elite and the media because they don't know what they're talking about and they have an agenda.

We must also be wary of the narrative that's being advanced by some in our own party, the notion that a Hillary Clinton administration wouldn't be that bad, that the effects would only be temporary. That it would only last for four and at most eight years. They're not using their God-given brain to think about what they're saying, because it won't be four or eight years, because she will be appointing people who will have an effect on us for generations and America may never recover from that. That's what we have to be thinking about.

Interestingly enough, we have to start thinking about what would Hillary Clinton do if she was, in fact, president. She would appoint Supreme Court justices, she would appoint federal judges, and that would have a deleterious effect on what happens for generations to come.

Not only that, but she would continue with a system that denigrates the education of our young people, puts them in a place where they're never going to be able to get a job, where they're always going to be dependent and where they can therefore be cultivated for their votes. This is not what America is all about, this kind of deception. And this is what we the people have the necessary obligation to fight.

One of the things that I have learned about Hillary Clinton is that one of her heroes, her mentors, was Saul Alinsky. Her senior thesis was about Saul Alinsky. This was someone that she greatly admired and that affected all of her philosophies subsequently. Now, interestingly enough, let me tell you something about Saul Alinsky.

He wrote a book called "Rules for Radicals." On the dedication page, it acknowledges Lucifer, the original radical who gained his own kingdom. Now think about that. This is a nation where our founding document, the Declaration of Independence, talks about certain inalienable rights that come from our creator. This is a nation where our Pledge of Allegiance says we are "one nation, under God."

This is a nation where every coin in our pocket and every bill in our wallet says, "In God We Trust." So are we willing to elect someone as president who has as their role model somebody who acknowledges Lucifer? Think about that.

The secular progressive agenda is antithetical to the principles of the founding of this nation. If we continue to allow them to take God out of our lives, God will remove himself from us, we will not be blessed, and our nation will go down the tubes and we will be responsible for that. We don't want that to happen.

Now Donald Trump, he understands this fairly well, he understands that the blessings of this nation come with the responsibility to ensure that they are available to all, not just the privileged few.

This is exemplified by his willingness to take on the establishment against all odds. It is evident in his passion for the American worker, it is found in his desire to put his considerable skills to work on behalf of American interests and not his self-interest. I'm proud to support Donald Trump, an extraordinary businessman, the right leader for a time such as this.

But you know what? It is not about Donald Trump. It is not about me. It is about we, the people, and Thomas Jefferson said that we would reach this point because we the people would not be paying attention and it would allow the government to grow, to expand, and to metastasize and to try to rule us. But he said before we turn into something else, we the people would recognize what was going on, what we were about to lose, and we would rise up and we would take control of our nation and I say now is the time for us to rise up and take America back.

Thank you, Dr. Carson for helping people know that America is in trouble; that Hillary Clinton was never the answer, and that Donald Trump was the best in this election and probably many more if he were available--besides yourself of course—to accomplish the mission of making America great again.

Chapter 13 Newt Gingrich, Friend of Donald Trump

Running America needs a great man!

No matter where he goes, Newt Gingrich is typically the smartest guy in the room. He is relied upon for counsel by many, including the news media who will never credit his sage, especially when they cannot figure something out.

Gingrich has a history of coming up with unique solutions to problems by pulling ideas from multiple unexpected places and putting them together for solutions that nobody else has ever come up with. When Republican naysayers were mocking Donald Trump's improbable White House campaign before the primaries started, Newt Gingrich was reading "Trump: The Art of the Deal."

It helped the Speaker get a perfect introduction to the real Trump -- and it was the beginning of an almost scholarly undertaking to understand the makings of the man who would go on to seize his party's nomination for president. Months later, as the GOP prepared to bring the nomination to Mr. Trump at its convention, the former House Speaker emerged as one of Trump's most high-profile supporters and even secured himself a top spot on the billionaire's vice-presidential shortlist.

Newt Gingrich is no fool and he knew and continues to know that Donald Trump, a man like all men, with faults, has qualities possessed by few. And, of course, guts is at the top of Trump's short list.

Having Newt Gingrich on your side is a big deal, Having Newt Gingrich give a speech for you at the Republican National Convention is a smart move. It is just another of many reasons Why Trump Got Elected!"

The Newt Gingrich RNC Speech

Former Speaker of the House Newt Gingrich spoke at the Republican National Convention Wednesday evening, introduced by his wife, Callista Gingrich. Here are his remarks as prepared:

And thank you, Callista. You know, she makes documentary films, and writes a best-selling children's series on American history. In addition, she sings in the Basilica Choir, and plays the French horn in the Fairfax Band. I am amazed at her achievements.

Tonight, I want to speak about a subject that has dominated my thinking for decades: How do we keep America safe?

There have been many fascinating things to watch about the extraordinary, historic rise of Donald Trump.

But the most significant has been Donald Trump's courage to tell some important truths about our national security.

For example:

- ✓ We are at War.
- ✓ We are at War with Radical Islamists.
- ✓ They are determined to kill us.
- ✓ They are stronger than we admit.
- ✓ And there is NO substitute for victory.

In contrast to Donald Trump, our national security and foreign policy elites, led by Hillary Clinton, are incapable of speaking with such honesty.

While *they* lie about the threat, *we* need to tell the truth about the danger.

If our enemies had their way, not a single woman in this room could define her future.

If our enemies had their way, gays, lesbians and transgender citizens would be put to death as they are today in the Islamic State and Iran.

If our enemies had their way, every person on earth would be subject to conversion by the sword and to a cruel and violent system of law.

There would be no individual liberty.

There would be no equality.

There would be no freedom.

If you doubt we are at war...

If you doubt that this threat is as real as I say...

Let me refresh your memory:

On Monday, an Afghan refugee in Germany used an axe and knives to slash and wound train passengers while shouting "Allahu Akbar."

Last week, ISIS claimed responsibility after a Tunisian man drove a cargo truck into a crowd in Nice, France. He murdered 84 people, including at least 10 children and three Americans, and injured over 300 others.

Two weeks ago, almost 300 people were killed and more than 200 were wounded in bombing attacks in Baghdad.

Two days before that, radical Islamists in Bangladesh killed 20 hostages, including 3 American college students.

A few days before that, at the Istanbul airport in Turkey, ISIS attackers armed with guns and bombs killed 44 people and injured hundreds more.

Last month, a radical Islamist in Paris stalked a French police officer to his home, where he murdered the officer and tortured his wife to death in front of their three-year-old son, while streaming it all on social media.

He was pondering whether to kill the three-year-old when he was killed by police.

Two days before that, an attacker pledging allegiance to ISIS killed 49 people in an Orlando nightclub and wounded dozens more.

All this in just the past *37 days*.

We *cannot* let ourselves grow numb to these accumulating atrocities.

One analysis estimated that since January of 2015, some 30,000 people have been killed at the hands of terrorists.

Donald Trump is right!

We are at war with radical Islamists, we are losing the war, and we must change course to win the war.

Let me be very clear, because I know the news media will do their best to distort this.

We have nothing to fear from the vast majority of Muslims in the United States, or around the world.

The vast majority are peaceful. They are often the *victims* of the violence themselves.

They are people we would be happy to have as our friends and neighbors.

The challenge is, when even a *small* percentage of a billion, six hundred million people support violence against those who disagree with them, that is still a *giant* recruiting base.

For example, Pew Research finds that just 9 percent of Muslims in Pakistan view ISIS favorably.

Unfortunately, 9 percent is 16 million people.

And that's just one country.

So, the truth is, although we are losing the war with radical Islamists, we have been very lucky.

The danger we face is much worse than the horrors that happened in Germany on New Year's Eve, when twelve-hundred women were assaulted.

It's worse than what's happening in France, where there are stabbings of Jews in the streets and the nation's security chief warned recently that France is "on the brink of civil war."

It's worse than what's happening in Israel, where average citizens fear for their lives whenever they leave their homes.

The danger is even worse than September 11th, when 19 hijackers murdered almost 3,000 Americans.

The *worst*-case scenario is losing an American city to terrorists armed with weapons of mass destruction.

Instead of losing 3,000 people in one morning, we could lose more than 300,000.

Instead of losing 2 great buildings, we could lose block after block after block to a nuclear event.

That's not just my view. Back in January of 2001, the Hart Rudman Commission warned that terrorists, "*will* acquire weapons of mass destruction... and some will use them.

Americans will likely die on American soil, possibly in large numbers."

15 years later, the dangers are even greater.

In a world where Pakistan has nuclear weapons... where North Korea has nuclear weapons... and where *Iran*--the world's leading state sponsor of terrorism--is close to having nuclear weapons... this, a *catastrophic* attack on innocent Americans, is a very real threat.

Which brings us to the heart of the matter.

We are sleepwalking through history as though this is All About Politics.

It is not.

It is about our safety and our survival as a country.

We *cannot* keep in place the people and the systems that have brought us to this point and that LIE to us every single day about the threat.

That is why every American should be terrified at the prospect of a Hillary Clinton presidency.

Hillary Clinton has been right at the center of this dishonesty. We know this administration and its allies lied to us about the Iran nuclear deal. We know it because they openly bragged about it to the New York Times.

We know that Hillary Clinton lied to us knowingly about the terror attack on our Benghazi consulate.

We know that Hillary Clinton and President Obama lie to the American people when they say they can safely screen the Syrian refugees. They *cannot*. And yet Hillary wants to increase the number by 500 percent.

So, when you hear about Hillary's dishonesty, or the emails, or taking millions from the Saudis and other Middle Eastern dictatorships-- remember: this is not about politics.

The cost of Hillary's dishonesty could be the loss of America as we know it.

The first step forward to safety is electing a leader who will be truthful with the American people about the realities we face.

Only then will we understand, support, and demand the strategies required to confront this threat.

And because safety and security are the preconditions for our freedom and prosperity, it is also the first step toward rebuilding the America we love.

Donald Trump understands this.

And that's why he will rebuild our military-- because he knows that a strong military is the best way to ensure peace.

Donald Trump will secure our borders-- because there is no such thing as a nation without a border.

Donald Trump will enforce our immigration laws. He will end the policy of deliberate non-enforcement and will end the abuse of our visa programs--to protect Americans workers, and their wages.

Donald Trump will take care of our veterans by holding bureaucrats at the Veterans Administration accountable. He will fire those responsible for the waiting lists, and will give veterans more choices about their care.

With Donald Trump's leadership, no bureaucrat will get between a veteran and their doctor.

Donald Trump will get America building again.

He *will* blow apart the ridiculous regulations and requirements that drive up infrastructure costs and drag out the timeline to get anything built.

The Trump Infrastructure program *will* make us once again the most competitive economy in the world.

Donald Trump *will* rebuild our education system, and give *every parent* of *every* income and *every* ethnic background a choice about where their children go to school.

And Donald Trump will help us rebuild and strengthen our communities.

Here again, the first step is safety-- the basis for strong families, and good jobs, and vibrant neighborhoods.

That means restoring law and order.

Donald Trump will show *zero* tolerance for people calling for the death of police officers.

Think about this. If anyone publicly threatens the life of the President of the United States, the Secret Service is on them in an instant.

Our law enforcement officers deserve the same respect.

And *of course*, if individual officers are found to have *violated* someone's rights, they *must* be held accountable under the law. America is *based* on the rule of law.

We are one nation, under God, indivisible with liberty and justice for *all*.

That is what has allowed us to absorb more people from more backgrounds than any nation in history.

Nobody is above the law. And nobody is too small to deserve its protection.

Donald Trump won our party's nomination because he is willing to tell the truth about the things that matter most.

He has a *great* running mate in Mike Pence.
They *will* put our safety first, and they will defend America first.

We can be proud to stand with them.

So tonight, the challenge for everyone in this hall, and everyone-- Republican, Democrat, or Independent--who is watching at home and knows we cannot continue on our current course...

...Is to rise above our factions, and rise above the politics we've inherited;

to ignore the lies of the news media and the old order;

to reject the suicidal *dishonesty* of Hillary Clinton and her establishment allies;

and to stand with Donald Trump and Mike Pence for what we know is true:

We *can* make America safe again;

We *can* make America work again;

We *can* make America first again;

And together, we *can* make America great again -- for *all* Americans.

Thank you and God Bless the United States of America.

I was in awe on this particular Wednesday watching Newt Gingrich deliver this historical speech. You have to love America and trust that your candidate loves America to deliver a speech as well as

Newt delivered this one. Democrats called it hatemongering but then again, they try to hide the truth from their minions so that they can help them continue being dependent on the government.

Thank you, Newt Gingrich. You would have been a worthy Vice President. I see you have a great advisory role in the Trump Administration. I appreciate all of your great work for President Trump as he and the rest of America appreciate your fine work on his behalf. You are most appreciated, sir!

The truth as delivered by Newt Gingrich and others in the many speeches given in support of Donald Trump's candidacy were a major contributory factor to **"Why Trump Got Elected!"**

Chapter 14 Donald Trump 45th US President—RNC Speech

Donald Trump at his absolute best!

Donald Trump showed energy and stamina and a definite love for addressing large crowds during his long, arduous and totally successful campaign for the presidency. The people loved him and he loved the people. That's "Why Trump Got Elected!"

If the coverage at his rallies by the corrupt press had been fair, all of America would have been as impressed as these typical supporters:

MrVegiita: You can hear the Power of Americans uniting behind Trump. Awesome coverage

The Frugal Gamer I was there it was amazing!

Daniel Bertola Hearing fellow Americans yelling U-S-A, U-S-A!!!!! So powerful. Gives me chills.

BlueGrassFan
This is why Trump is going to win by a landslide.
Peter Spiderman Wow! the crowd was awesome...full of energy. Money can't buy support. Trump is genuine. He just came at the right time, at the right moment..

Društveni Dokaz: I'm not American (at least not yet), but I would really like to see Donald Trump as the POTUS.

Jason Vylášek: My God!!!!!! Clinton has like 7 people sitting in chairs drinking tea at her rallies. This is a brutal beat down. She's had it long coming!

ElectricJohnny: This isn't a one off. Trump fills stadiums every day. This is a revolution.

Arthur Trella: Nice crowd. So glad trump won big time!

Zirasayers: Trump rallies are like Rock Concerts!! Donald Trump is truly amazing. He flies all over the country to bring Americans together again and usually does 1 rally a day if not 2 rallies. Unlike Hillary Clinton who is almost never seen in public, continuously cancels her events probably due to her failing health, and only wants to divide everyone up by race and gender. Not to mention her endless list of scandals over her 30 year of politics.

…

That's "Why Trump Was Elected!"

The following Remarks at the RNC were transcribed as prepared for delivery according to a draft obtained by POLITICO Thursday July 21 afternoon.

Friends, delegates and fellow Americans: I humbly and gratefully accept your nomination for the presidency of the United States.

Together, we will lead our party back to the White House, and we will lead our country back to safety, prosperity, and peace. We will be a country of generosity and warmth. But we will also be a country of law and order.

Our Convention occurs at a moment of crisis for our nation. The attacks on our police, and the terrorism in our cities, threaten our very way of life. Any politician who does not grasp this danger is not fit to lead our country.

Americans watching this address tonight have seen the recent images of violence in our streets and the chaos in our communities. Many have witnessed this violence personally, some have even been its victims.

I have a message for all of you: the crime and violence that today afflicts our nation will soon come to an end. Beginning on January 20th 2017, safety will be restored.

The most basic duty of government is to defend the lives of its own citizens. Any government that fails to do so is a government unworthy to lead.

It is finally time for a straightforward assessment of the state of our nation.
I will present the facts plainly and honestly. We cannot afford to be so politically correct anymore.

So, if you want to hear the corporate spin, the carefully-crafted lies, and the media myths the Democrats are holding their convention next week.

But here, at our convention, there will be no lies. We will honor the American people with the truth, and nothing else.

Decades of progress made in bringing down crime are now being reversed by this Administration's rollback of criminal enforcement.

Homicides last year increased by 17% in America's fifty largest cities. That's the largest increase in 25 years. In our nation's capital, killings have risen by 50 percent. They are up nearly 60% in nearby Baltimore.

In the President's hometown of Chicago, more than 2,000 have been the victims of shootings this year alone. And more than 3,600 have been killed in the Chicago area since he took office.

The number of police officers killed in the line of duty has risen by almost 50% compared to this point last year. Nearly 180,000 illegal immigrants with criminal records, ordered deported from our country, are tonight roaming free to threaten peaceful citizens.

The number of new illegal immigrant families who have crossed the border so far this year already exceeds the entire total from 2015. They are being released by the tens of thousands into our communities with no regard for the impact on public safety or resources.

One such border-crosser was released and made his way to Nebraska. There, he ended the life of an innocent young girl named Sarah Root. She was 21 years-old, and was killed the day after graduating from college with a 4.0 Grade Point Average. Her killer was then released a second time, and he is now a fugitive from the law.

I've met Sarah's beautiful family. But to this Administration, their amazing daughter was just one more American life that wasn't worth protecting. One more child to sacrifice on the altar of open borders. What about our economy?

Again, I will tell you the plain facts that have been edited out of your nightly news and your morning newspaper: Nearly Four in 10 African-American children are living in poverty, while 58% of African

American youth are not employed. 2 million more Latinos are in poverty today than when the President took his oath of office less than eight years ago. Another 14 million people have left the workforce entirely.

Household incomes are down more than $4,000 since the year 2000. Our manufacturing trade deficit has reached an all-time high – nearly $800 billion in a single year. The budget is no better.

President Obama has doubled our national debt to more than $19 trillion, and growing. Yet, what do we have to show for it? Our roads and bridges are falling apart, our airports are in Third World condition, and forty-three million Americans are on food stamps.

Now let us consider the state of affairs abroad.
Not only have our citizens endured domestic disaster, but they have lived through one international humiliation after another. We all remember the images of our sailors being forced to their knees by their Iranian captors at gunpoint.

This was just prior to the signing of the Iran deal, which gave back to Iran $150 billion and gave us nothing – it will go down in history as one of the worst deals ever made. Another humiliation came when president Obama drew a red line in Syria – and the whole world knew it meant nothing.

In Libya, our consulate – the symbol of American prestige around the globe – was brought down in flames. America is far less safe – and the world is far less stable – than when Obama made the decision to put Hillary Clinton in charge of America's foreign policy.

I am certain it is a decision he truly regrets. Her bad instincts and her bad judgment – something pointed out by Bernie Sanders – are what caused the disasters unfolding today. Let's review the record. In 2009, pre-Hillary, ISIS was not even on the map.

Libya was cooperating. Egypt was peaceful. Iraq was seeing a reduction in violence. Iran was being choked by sanctions. Syria was under control. After four years of Hillary Clinton, what do we have? ISIS has spread across the region, and the world. Libya is in ruins, and our Ambassador and his staff were left helpless to die at the hands of savage killers. Egypt was turned over to the radical Muslim brotherhood, forcing the military to retake control. Iraq is in chaos.

Iran is on the path to nuclear weapons. Syria is engulfed in a civil war and a refugee crisis that now threatens the West. After fifteen years of wars in the Middle East, after trillions of dollars spent and thousands of lives lost, the situation is worse than it has ever been before.

This is the legacy of Hillary Clinton: death, destruction and weakness.

But Hillary Clinton's legacy does not have to be America's legacy. The problems we face now – poverty and violence at home, war and destruction abroad – will last only as long as we continue relying on the same politicians who created them. A change in leadership is required to change these outcomes. Tonight, I will share with you my plan of action for America.

The most important difference between our plan and that of our opponents, is that our plan will put America First. Americanism, not globalism, will be our credo. As long as we are led by politicians who will not put America First, then we can be assured that other nations will not treat America with respect. This will all change in 2017.

The American People will come first once again. My plan will begin with safety at home – which means safe neighborhoods, secure borders, and protection from terrorism. There can be no prosperity without law and order. On the economy, I will outline reforms to add millions of new jobs and trillions in new wealth that can be used to rebuild America.

A number of these reforms that I will outline tonight will be opposed by some of our nation's most powerful special interests. That is because these interests have rigged our political and economic system for their exclusive benefit.

Big business, elite media and major donors are lining up behind the campaign of my opponent because they know she will keep our rigged system in place. They are throwing money at her because they have total control over everything she does. She is their puppet, and they pull the strings.

That is why Hillary Clinton's message is that things will never change. My message is that things have to change – and they have to change right now. Every day I wake up determined to deliver for the people I have met all across this nation that have been neglected, ignored, and abandoned.

I have visited the laid-off factory workers, and the communities crushed by our horrible and unfair trade deals. These are the forgotten men and women of our country. People who work hard but no longer have a voice.

I AM YOUR VOICE.

I have embraced crying mothers who have lost their children because our politicians put their personal agendas before the national good. I have no patience for injustice, no tolerance for government incompetence, no sympathy for leaders who fail their citizens.

When innocent people suffer, because our political system lacks the will, or the courage, or the basic decency to enforce our laws – or worse still, has sold out to some corporate lobbyist for cash – I am not able to look the other way.

And when a Secretary of State illegally stores her emails on a private server, deletes 33,000 of them so the authorities can't see her crime, puts our country at risk, lies about it in every different form and faces no consequence – I know that corruption has reached a level like never before.

When the FBI Director says that the Secretary of State was "extremely careless" and "negligent," in handling our classified secrets, I also know that these terms are minor compared to what she actually did. They were just used to save her from facing justice for her terrible crimes.

In fact, her single greatest accomplishment may be committing such an egregious crime and getting away with it – especially when others have paid so dearly. When that same Secretary of State rakes in millions of dollars trading access, and favors to special interests and foreign powers I know the time for action has come.

I have joined the political arena so that the powerful can no longer beat up on people that cannot defend themselves. Nobody knows the system better than me, which is why I alone can fix it. I have seen firsthand how the system is rigged against our citizens, just like it was rigged against Bernie Sanders – he never had a chance.

But his supporters will join our movement, because we will fix his biggest issue: trade. Millions of Democrats will join our movement because we are going to fix the system, so it works for all Americans. In this cause, I am proud to have at my side the next Vice President of the United States: Governor Mike Pence of Indiana.

We will bring the same economic success to America that Mike brought to Indiana. He is a man of character and accomplishment. He is the right man for the job. The first task for our new Administration will be to liberate our citizens from the crime and terrorism and lawlessness that threatens their communities.

America was shocked to its core when our police officers in Dallas were brutally executed. In the days after Dallas, we have seen continued threats and violence against our law enforcement officials. Law officers have been shot or killed in recent days in Georgia, Missouri, Wisconsin, Kansas, Michigan and Tennessee.

On Sunday, more police were gunned down in Baton Rouge, Louisiana. Three were killed, and four were badly injured. An attack on law enforcement is an attack on all Americans. I have a message to every last person threatening the peace on our streets and the safety of our police: when I take the oath of office next year, I will restore law and order our country.

I will work with, and appoint, the best prosecutors and law enforcement officials in the country to get the job done. In this race for the White House, I am the Law and Order candidate. The irresponsible rhetoric of our President, who has used the pulpit of the presidency to divide us by race and color, has made America a more dangerous environment for everyone.

This Administration has failed America's inner cities. It's failed them on education. It's failed them on jobs. It's failed them on crime. It's failed them at every level.
When I am President, I will work to ensure that all of our kids are treated equally, and protected equally.

Every action I take, I will ask myself: does this make life better for young Americans in Baltimore, Chicago, Detroit, Ferguson who have as much of a right to live out their dreams as any other child America?

To make life safe in America, we must also address the growing threats we face from outside America: we are going to defeat the barbarians of ISIS. Once again, France is the victim of brutal Islamic terrorism.

Men, women and children viciously mowed down. Lives ruined. Families ripped apart. A nation in mourning.

The damage and devastation that can be inflicted by Islamic radicals has been over and over – at the World Trade Center, at an office party in San Bernardino, at the Boston Marathon, and a military recruiting center in Chattanooga, Tennessee.

Only weeks ago, in Orlando, Florida, 49 wonderful Americans were savagely murdered by an Islamic terrorist. This time, the terrorist targeted our LGBT community. As your President, I will do everything in my power to protect our LGBT citizens from the violence and oppression of a hateful foreign ideology. To protect us from terrorism, we need to focus on three things.

We must have the best intelligence gathering operation in the world. We must abandon the failed policy of nation building and regime change that Hillary Clinton pushed in Iraq, Libya, Egypt and Syria. Instead, we must work with all of our allies who share our goal of destroying ISIS and stamping out Islamic terror.

This includes working with our greatest ally in the region, the State of Israel. Lastly, we must immediately suspend immigration from any nation that has been compromised by terrorism until such time as proven vetting mechanisms have been put in place.

My opponent has called for a radical 550% increase in Syrian refugees on top of existing massive refugee flows coming into our country under President Obama. She proposes this despite the fact that there's no way to screen these refugees in order to find out who they are or where they come from. I only want to admit individuals into our country who will support our values and love our people.

Anyone who endorses violence, hatred or oppression is not welcome in our country and never will be.

Decades of record immigration have produced lower wages and higher unemployment for our citizens, especially for African-American and Latino workers. We are going to have an immigration system that works, but one that works for the American people.

On Monday, we heard from three parents whose children were killed by illegal immigrants Mary Ann Mendoza, Sabine Durden, and Jamiel Shaw. They are just three brave representatives of many thousands. Of all my travels in this country, nothing has affected me more deeply than the time I have spent with the mothers and fathers who have lost their children to violence spilling across our border.

These families have no special interests to represent them. There are no demonstrators to protest on their behalf. My opponent will never meet with them, or share in their pain. Instead, my opponent wants Sanctuary Cities. But where was sanctuary for Kate Steinle? Where was sanctuary for the children of Mary Ann, Sabine and Jamiel? Where was sanctuary for all the other Americans who have been so brutally murdered, and who have suffered so horribly?

These wounded American families have been alone. But they are alone no longer. Tonight, this candidate and this whole nation stand in their corner to support them, to send them our love, and to pledge in their honor that we will save countless more families from suffering the same awful fate.

We are going to build a great border wall to stop illegal immigration, to stop the gangs and the violence, and to stop the drugs from pouring into our communities. I have been honored to receive the endorsement of America's Border Patrol Agents, and will work directly with them to protect the integrity of our lawful immigration system.

By ending catch-and-release on the border, we will stop the cycle of human smuggling and violence. Illegal border crossings will go down. Peace will be restored. By enforcing the rules for the millions who overstay their visas, our laws will finally receive the respect they deserve.

Tonight, I want every American whose demands for immigration security have been denied – and every politician who has denied them – to listen very closely to the words I am about to say.

On January 21st of 2017, the day after I take the oath of office, Americans will finally wake up in a country where the laws of the

United States are enforced. We are going to be considerate and compassionate to everyone.

But my greatest compassion will be for our own struggling citizens. My plan is the exact opposite of the radical and dangerous immigration policy of Hillary Clinton. Americans want relief from uncontrolled immigration. Communities want relief.

Yet Hillary Clinton is proposing mass amnesty, mass immigration, and mass lawlessness. Her plan will overwhelm your schools and hospitals, further reduce your jobs and wages, and make it harder for recent immigrants to escape from poverty.

I have a different vision for our workers. It begins with a new, fair trade policy that protects our jobs and stands up to countries that cheat. It's been a signature message of my campaign from day one, and it will be a signature feature of my presidency from the moment I take the oath of office.

I have made billions of dollars in business making deals – now I'm going to make our country rich again. I am going to turn our bad trade agreements into great ones.

America has lost nearly-one third of its manufacturing jobs since 1997, following the enactment of disastrous trade deals supported by Bill and Hillary Clinton.

Remember, it was Bill Clinton who signed NAFTA, one of the worst economic deals ever made by our country.

Never again.

I am going to bring our jobs back to Ohio and to America – and I am not going to let companies move to other countries, firing their employees along the way, without consequences.

My opponent, on the other hand, has supported virtually every trade agreement that has been destroying our middle class. She supported NAFTA, and she supported China's entrance into the World Trade Organization – another one of her husband's colossal mistakes.

She supported the job killing trade deal with South Korea. She has supported the Trans-Pacific Partnership. The TPP will not only destroy our manufacturing, but it will make America subject to the rulings of foreign governments. I pledge to never sign any trade agreement that hurts our workers, or that diminishes our freedom and independence.

Instead, I will make individual deals with individual countries.

No longer will we enter into these massive deals, with many countries, that are thousands of pages long – and which no one from our country even reads or understands. We are going to enforce all trade violations, including through the use of taxes and tariffs, against any country that cheats.

This includes stopping China's outrageous theft of intellectual property, along with their illegal product dumping, and their devastating currency manipulation. Our horrible trade agreements with China and many others, will be totally renegotiated. That includes renegotiating NAFTA to get a much better deal for America – and we'll walk away if we don't get the deal that we want. We are going to start building and making things again.

Next comes the reform of our tax laws, regulations and energy rules. While Hillary Clinton plans a massive tax increase, I have proposed the largest tax reduction of any candidate who has declared for the presidential race this year – Democrat or Republican. Middle-income Americans will experience profound relief, and taxes will be simplified for everyone.

America is one of the highest-taxed nations in the world. Reducing taxes will cause new companies and new jobs to come roaring back into our country. Then we are going to deal with the issue of regulation, one of the greatest job-killers of them all. Excessive regulation is costing our country as much as $2 trillion a year, and we will end it. We are going to lift the restrictions on the production of American energy. This will produce more than $20 trillion in job creating economic activity over the next four decades.

My opponent, on the other hand, wants to put the great miners and steel workers of our country out of work – that will never happen when I am President. With these new economic policies, trillions of dollars will start flowing into our country.

This new wealth will improve the quality of life for all Americans – We will build the roads, highways, bridges, tunnels, airports, and the railways of tomorrow. This, in turn, will create millions more jobs. We will rescue kids from failing schools by helping their parents send them to a safe school of their choice.

My opponent would rather protect education bureaucrats than serve American children. We will repeal and replace disastrous Obamacare. You will be able to choose your own doctor again. And we will fix TSA at the airports! We will completely rebuild our depleted military, and the countries that we protect, at a massive loss, will be asked to pay their fair share.

We will take care of our great Veterans like they have never been taken care of before.

My opponent dismissed the VA scandal as being not widespread – one more sign of how out of touch she really is. We are going to ask every Department Head in government to provide a list of wasteful spending projects that we can eliminate in my first 100 days. The politicians have talked about it, I'm going to do it. We are also going to appoint justices to the United States Supreme Court who will uphold our laws and our Constitution.

The replacement for Justice Scalia will be a person of similar views and principles. This will be one of the most important issues decided by this election. My opponent wants to essentially abolish the 2nd amendment. I, on the other hand, received the early and strong endorsement of the National Rifle Association and will protect the right of all Americans to keep their families safe.

At this moment, I would like to thank the evangelical community who have been so good to me and so supportive. You have so much to contribute to our politics, yet our laws prevent you from speaking your minds from your own pulpits.

An amendment, pushed by Lyndon Johnson, many years ago, threatens religious institutions with a loss of their tax-exempt status if they openly advocate their political views.

I am going to work very hard to repeal that language and protect free speech for all Americans. We can accomplish these great things, and so much else – all we need to do is start believing in ourselves and in our country again. It is time to show the whole world that America Is Back – bigger, and better and stronger than ever before.

In this journey, I'm so lucky to have at my side my wife Melania and my wonderful children, Don, Ivanka, Eric, Tiffany, and Barron: you will always be my greatest source of pride and joy. My Dad, Fred Trump, was the smartest and hardest working man I ever knew. I wonder sometimes what he'd say if he were here to see this tonight.

It's because of him that I learned, from my youngest age, to respect the dignity of work and the dignity of working people. He was a guy most comfortable in the company of bricklayers, carpenters, and electricians and I have a lot of that in me also. Then there's my mother, Mary. She was strong, but also warm and fair-minded. She was a truly great mother. She was also one of the most honest and charitable people I have ever known, and a great judge of character.

To my sisters Mary Anne and Elizabeth, my brother Robert and my late brother Fred, I will always give you my love you are most special to me. I have loved my life in business.

But now, my sole and exclusive mission is to go to work for our country – to go to work for all of you. It's time to deliver a victory for the American people. But to do that, we must break free from the petty politics of the past.

America is a nation of believers, dreamers, and strivers that is being led by a group of censors, critics, and cynics.

Remember: all of the people telling you that you can't have the country you want, are the same people telling you that I wouldn't be standing here tonight. No longer can we rely on those elites in media, and politics, who will say anything to keep a rigged system in place.

Instead, we must choose to Believe in America. History is watching us now.

It's waiting to see if we will rise to the occasion, and if we will show the whole world that America is still free and independent and strong.

My opponent asks her supporters to recite a three-word loyalty pledge. It reads: "I'm With Her". I choose to recite a different pledge.

My pledge reads: "I'M WITH YOU – THE AMERICAN PEOPLE."

I am your voice.

So to every parent who dreams for their child, and every child who dreams for their future, I say these words to you tonight: I'm With You, and I will fight for you, and I will win for you.

To all Americans tonight, in all our cities and towns, I make this promise:

We Will Make America Strong Again.

We Will Make America Proud Again.

We Will Make America Safe Again.

And We Will Make America Great Again.

THANK YOU.

That says it all folks and that is:

"Why Trump Got Elected!"

Thank you for choosing this book to help you better understand

"Why Trump Got Elected!"

It still is a great feeling, is it not?

Other books by Brian Kelly: (amazon.com, and Kindle)

Taxation Without Representation Can the US Afford Another Tea Party?
Delete the EPA You won't believe what they are up to now!
Wipe Out All Student Debt Now! How to improve the economy with one bold move
 Boost Social Security Now! Hey Buddy Can You Spare a Dime?
The Birth of American Football. From the first college game in 1869 to the last Super Bowl
Obamacare: A One-Line Repeal Congress must get this done.
A Wilkes-Barre Christmas Story A wonderful town makes Christmas all the better
A Boy, A Bike, A Train, and a Christmas Miracle a Christmas story that will melt your heart
Pay-to-Go   America-First Immigration Fix
Legalizing Illegal Aliens Via Resident Visas Americans-first plan saves $Trillions. Learn how!
60 Million Illegal Aliens in America!!! A simple, America-first solution.
The Bill of Rights by Founder James Madison Refresh *your knowledge of the specific rights for all*
It's time for the John Doe Party! Republicans can no longer handle the load.
Great Players in Army Football Great Army Football played by great players..
Great Coaches in Army Football Army's coaches are all great.
Great Moments in Army Football Army Football at its best.
Great Moments in Florida Gators Football Gators Football from the start. This is the book.
Great Moments in Clemson Football CU Football at its best. This is the book.
Great Moments in Florida Gators Football Gators Football from the start. This is the book.
The **Constitution Companion.** A Guide to Reading and Comprehending the Constitution
The Constitution by Hamilton, Jefferson, & Madison – Big type and in English
PATERNO: The Dark Days After Win # 409. Sky began to fall within days of win # 409.
JoePa 409 Victories: Say No More! Winningest Division I-A football coach ever
American College Football: The Beginning From before day one football was played.
Great Coaches in Alabama Football Challenging the coaches of every other program!
Great Coaches in Penn State Football the Best Coaches in PSU's football program
Great Players in Penn State Football The best players in PSU's football program
Great Players in Notre Dame Football The best players in ND's football program
Great Coaches in Notre Dame Football The best coaches in any football program
Great Players in Alabama Football from Quarterbacks to offensive Linemen Greats!
Great Moments in Alabama Football AU Football from the start. This is the book.
Great Moments in Penn State Football PSU Football, start--games, coaches, players,
Great Moments in Notre Dame Football ND Football, start, games, coaches, players
Cross Country With the Parents A great trip from East Coast to West with the kids
Seniors, Social Security & the Minimum Wage. Things seniors need to know.
How to Write Your First Book and Publish It with CreateSpace
The US Immigration Fix--It's all in here. Finally, an answer.
I had a Dream IBM Could be #1 Again The title is self-explanatory
WineDiets.Com Presents The Wine Diet Learn how to lose weight while having fun.
Wilkes-Barre, PA; Return to Glory Wilkes-Barre City's return to glory
Geoffrey Parsons' Epoch... The Land of Fair Play Better than the original.
The Bill of Rights 4 Dummmies! This is the best book to learn about your rights.
Sol Bloom's Epoch …Story of the Constitution The best book to learn the Constitution
America 4 Dummmies! All Americans should read to learn about this great country.
The Electoral College 4 Dummmies! How does it really work?
The All-Everything Machine Story about IBM's finest computer server.
ThankYou IBM! This book explains how IBM was beaten in the computer marketplace by neophytes

Brian has written 146 books in total. Other books can be found at amazon.com/author/brianwkelly

www.ingramcontent.com/pod-product-compliance
Lightning Source LLC
Chambersburg PA
CBHW060859280326
41934CB00007B/1107